nt to be a chef
AROUND
HE WORLD

# I want to be a chef
# AROUND
# THE WORLD

MURDOCH BOOKS

# contents

# let's cook ...

What better way to travel and experience the variety of wonderful flavours in the world than through your own kitchen. From the traditional flavours of Italy, to the exotic spices of Morocco and the simple art of Japanese sushi-making, this book will take you on a culinary trip to explore and discover authentic dishes from many parts of the globe.

## How to start

To be a successful cook, you must be organised. To produce the best results, a professional chef relies on a well-run, clean and tidy kitchen, and you should, too. Here are some important things you need to know before you start that will help to make cooking a real pleasure.

◆ First, read all the way through the recipe and check the list of ingredients to make sure you have everything you need before you start. Having to run to the shops in the middle of making a cake is not a good idea.

◆ If you are unfamiliar with an ingredient, cooking term or technique turn to the glossary (see page 184–7) for a quick explanation.

◆ Have the right equipment close to hand. Put the kitchen scales out on the kitchen bench. Have wooden spoons and knives set out in a row so they are in easy reach when you need them.

◆ Prepare any baking trays, tins or moulds at the beginning as the recipe instructs. They may need to be greased with oil or butter, and often will also need to be lined with baking paper, to make sure your cakes and biscuits don't stick.

◆ Before you start cooking, set out all the ingredients on the kitchen bench. Open tins, peel and chop fruit and vegetables as instructed, grate cheese and measure out amounts of flour, sugar and butter. Otherwise, you will have to stop and start frequently, which can take time and create a mess. Be sure to clean up as you go.

◆ Preheat the oven when the recipe tells you to.

◆ Read the recipe as you go and check that you're adding the ingredients in the right order.

◆ Be sure to have a kitchen timer with an alarm function or have a clock handy, to keep track of cooking times. It's easy to forget when you put something in the oven and baked items can easily overcook if left for too long.

## How to weigh and measure

It is very important that you measure ingredients carefully. The proportion of butter to flour, sugar to butter and so on is very precise, especially in baking cakes and making pastries. The end result can be badly affected if you don't follow the recipe.

Three different scales for measuring are given in the recipes: these are metric, imperial and cup measures. Whichever scale you use, stay with it throughout a recipe. If you like to measure in cups, stay with cups where possible. If you prefer to weigh things in grams, use grams to measure all the ingredients within each recipe.

You will need:
◆ a set of dry measuring cups, usually in a set of four: 250 ml (9 fl oz/1 cup), 125 ml (4 fl oz/½ cup), 80 ml (2½ fl oz/⅓ cup) and 60 ml (2 fl oz/¼ cup) measures. These are used for ingredients such as flour and sugar.

◆ a liquid measuring cup with a lip. This should have lines on the side that clearly show the measures.

◆ a set of measuring spoons: 1 tablespoon, 1 teaspoon, ½ teaspoon and ¼ teaspoon. You can buy metal or plastic ones.

Liquid measures
Put the measuring cup on the bench, then add some of the liquid and bend down so your eyes are level with the measurement marks. Check if you have too much or too little liquid and add or remove, as needed.

### Chopping boards

When you have chopped raw meat, chicken or seafood on a board, you must scrub the board and the knife in very hot water with detergent before using them for any other ingredients. Ask an adult to help; you must take care not to scald your hands. Ideally, have three boards: one for raw meat, chicken and fish, one for fruit and one for vegetables.

Dry measures
Spoon dry ingredients into the measuring cup or spoon and then level them off with a knife or metal spatula. Cup and spoon measures for dry ingredients should be level, not heaped (unless the recipe says otherwise).

## How to use the oven

If you're using the oven, place the shelves at the correct height before you turn it on. Always preheat the oven to the temperature given in the recipe before putting things in to cook. Most ovens have a light to show when the right temperature has been reached and you can put the food in.

If you have a fan-forced oven (ask an adult, if you're not sure), then the temperature will be a bit hotter than a normal oven. The temperatures given in the recipes in this book are for a normal oven. If you use a fan-forced oven, you will need to reduce the temperature for each recipe by about 20°C (35°F). This is most important for baking cakes, slices and cookies and other sweet things. It is less important for things such as roasts.

## Presentation

If you watch cooking programs on the television, you'll know that professional chefs always arrange food on the plate in an attractive way. While you don't need to spend a lot of time doing this (hot food will go cold if you fiddle around too long), it does add to the pleasure of eating if the food is arranged neatly and not just plopped on in a messy way. After all the trouble you've taken to cook something well, it makes sense to 'plate' it properly.

Setting the table is also important — it is much like setting the scene for a play. If the things surrounding the food complement each other the whole experience will be more enjoyable and memorable. Choose your serving plates, bowls and platters, cutlery and glassware carefully. Use your imagination and your food as inspiration when setting the table. You may like to select chopsticks and bowls with Asian-like patterns to serve your Singapore noodles, or set the table with red, white and green napkins (to represent the Italian flag) when serving lasagne, or use a vibrant coloured, sari-like fabric as a table cloth when you serve an Indian curry.

## Food safety

Knowing how to store and transport food safely is very important. Spoiled food can make you ill. While there is less to worry about with baked goods such as cakes, it is important to know how to handle raw products such as meat and chicken, which you may use in a pie or some other baked dish.

### How to handle uncooked meat

◆ As a general rule, raw meat will keep for up to 3 days in the fridge and up to 6 months in the freezer.

◆ To freeze meat, wrap each piece in plastic wrap, then put it in a freezer bag. Make sure that you get all the air out of the bag. Ask an adult if you need help. Label and date the bag because, once something is frozen, it is sometimes impossible to recognise what it is.

◆ To thaw, put the meat on a large plate and leave it in the fridge. Allow enough time for it to defrost fully before cooking. If you're not sure, ask an adult. Depending on how big the item is, it can take several hours or even overnight. Never thaw meat at room temperature or under water. Don't re-freeze thawed meat unless you have cooked it first.

### How to handle uncooked chicken

Chicken should be treated very carefully as it can harbour dangerous bacteria.

◆ Keep raw chicken in the fridge for 2 days, or up to 6 months in the freezer.

◆ Thaw chicken in the same way as meat. Cook it within 12 hours of thawing. Never let raw chicken (or other raw meat) come in contact with other foods in the fridge.

### How to handle cooked food

◆ Hot food that needs to be stored should be cooled quickly. Cover it and refrigerate as soon as the steam has stopped rising.

### Food allergies

Some people have an allergy to a particular food and may become very ill if they eat it. If you're having friends round for something to eat, ask an adult in the family to find out if any of them has a food intolerance, so you don't include an ingredient it is dangerous for them to eat. If someone has a severe nut allergy (to peanuts, for example), make sure there are no foods containing even the tiniest amount. Don't serve nuts or small sweets to children under five; they could choke on them.

◆ Make sure that food is completely cooked through. This is most important for chicken and minced (ground) meat.

◆ When you're reheating food, make sure it's warmed through before you serve it and isn't hot on the outside but still cold in the middle. If you're using a microwave, make sure you stir the food while reheating so it heats evenly.

◆ If you're packing food into a lunchbox, use one that's insulated or add a freezer pack. Don't pack hot foods in your lunchbox. First let them cool in the fridge.

## Top tips in the kitchen

1   Always ask an adult for permission before you start to cook. And always ask for help if you are not confident with chopping or handling hot cake tins.

2   Before you start, wash your hands well with soap and water, tie back long hair and wear an apron to protect your clothes. Have clean, dry oven gloves and tea towels (dish towels) handy.

3   Always wear closed-in shoes when in the kitchen. Always use thick, dry oven gloves when getting things out of the oven.

4   When cooking on the stovetop, turn pan handles to the side so there's no danger of knocking them. When you are stirring, hold the pan handle firmly.

5   Never use electrical appliances near water. Always dry your hands carefully before you touch any appliance. When you have finished with it, switch it off at the power point and remove the plug from the wall before cleaning it.

6   Turn off the oven, hotplate or gas ring when you have finished using it.

## How to use this book

All the recipes are broken down into a few simple steps. All of them have photographs so you can see what your finished product is going to look like. Some of the recipes have step-by-step photographs to help you with any techniques you may not be familiar with or have never tried before.

*And, finally ... have fun cooking and enjoy your journey to becoming a top-notch international chef.*

start the day

# bircher muesli

**SWITZERLAND** This popular cereal was first created around 1900 by a Swiss doctor who wanted to provide a healthy breakfast for hospital patients — it doesn't taste like hospital food though! Bircher muesli is also delicious served with blueberries or sliced bananas.

150 g (5½ oz/1½ cups) rolled (porridge) oats

300 ml (10½ fl oz) milk

200 g (7 oz) plain yoghurt

40 g (1½ oz/⅓ cup) sultanas (golden raisins)

1 large green apple

1 tablespoon sunflower seeds

2 tablespoons slivered almonds, toasted

SERVES 4–6

1 Combine the oats, milk, yoghurt and sultanas in a large bowl. Cover with plastic wrap and place in the refrigerator overnight.

2 In the morning, quarter and core the apple (leave the skin on) and then coarsely grate. Stir the grated apple, sunflower seeds and slivered almonds into the oat mixture. Serve the muesli topped with raspberries and honey.

# porridge

**SCOTLAND** Porridge is the traditional breakfast dish in Scotland. They love it so much that they even hold a World Porridge Making Championship every year to showcase the art of making porridge!

150 g (5½ oz/1½ cups) rolled (porridge) oats

375 ml (13 fl oz/1½ cups) milk

SERVES 4

1 Put the oats in a heavy-based saucepan with the milk, 500 ml (17 fl oz/2 cups) water and a pinch of salt. Stir over medium heat until it starts to simmer.

2 Reduce the heat and simmer for 10 minutes, stirring occasionally, or until creamy and the oats are tender.

3 Spoon the porridge into serving bowls. Serve with slices of banana, a drizzle of honey and some extra milk.

# quick welsh rarebit soldier toast

**WALES** This dish was originally called Welsh rabbit, but it was written incorrectly in a slang dictionary in 1785 and the misspelling of 'rarebit' stuck. Nobody knows why it was called Welsh either — some believe it may be because the Welsh were so poor they couldn't afford meat (rabbit was known as the poor man's meat), so they used cheese instead.

80 g (2¾ oz/⅔ cup) grated cheddar cheese

1 teaspoon mild English mustard

1 egg yolk

60 ml (2 fl oz/¼ cup) thickened (whipping) cream

4 eggs, at room temperature

4 thick slices white bread

2 teaspoons Worcestershire sauce, or to taste

SERVES 4

1 Preheat the grill (broiler) to high.

2 Mix together the cheese, mustard, egg yolk and cream in a bowl. Season with salt and black pepper.

3 Fill a medium saucepan with water and bring to the boil over high heat. Use a spoon to carefully lower the eggs, one at a time, into the water. Boil gently for 4 minutes for a soft-boiled egg.

4 Meanwhile, toast the bread lightly. Spread the cheese mixture evenly over the toast and then place on an oven tray. Cook under the preheated grill for 3 minutes, or until the cheese is bubbling and golden brown. Cut each slice into three wide strips and sprinkle the Worcestershire sauce over the top.

5 To serve, place the eggs into egg cups and slice the tops open with a knife or teaspoon. Dip the Welsh rarebit soldier toast into the egg.

# vietnamese omelette

**VIETNAM**  The French influence on Vietnamese cuisine is evident in this delicious breakfast omelette. The traditional Vietnamese flavours, including fragrant herbs, bean sprouts and *nuoc cham* (a popular dipping sauce), give this French favourite a new twist.

8 eggs

5 spring onions (scallions), thinly sliced

1 tablespoon oyster sauce

1 tablespoon finely chopped mint leaves

1 tablespoon finely chopped coriander (cilantro)

1 tablespoon peanut oil

90 g (3¼ oz/1 cup) bean sprouts, trimmed

### *Nuoc cham*

2 tablespoons Vietnamese fish sauce (see note)

2 teaspoons lime juice

1 teaspoon rice wine vinegar

1 teaspoon caster (superfine) sugar

1 long fresh red chilli, sliced

1 garlic clove, crushed

SERVES 4

1  Whisk together 2 of the eggs with ¼ of the spring onion and 1 teaspoon of the oyster sauce. Add ¼ of the mint and ¼ of the coriander and whisk until combined.

2  To make the *nuoc cham*, combine all the ingredients with 1 tablespoon water in a small bowl and set aside.

3  Heat 1 teaspoon of the oil in a small non-stick frying pan over medium heat. Add the egg mixture, tilting the pan to cover the base, and cook until almost set.

4  Sprinkle ¼ of the sprouts evenly over half of the omelette. Fold the omelette over to enclose the sprouts, then slide onto a plate. Repeat with the remaining ingredients to make three more omelettes. Serve with the *nuoc cham* sauce.

**Note:** Vietnamese fish sauce, labelled *nuoc nam*, is lighter than other fish sauces, and has a more subtle flavour.

# potato and carrot rösti with fried egg

**SWITZERLAND** Many Swiss farmers begin their day with a rösti (a traditional savoury pancake made with grated potato and onion) topped with a fried egg and a cup of milky coffee. We have added shredded carrot to our rösti to give a little sweetness and colour.

1 kg (2 lb 4 oz) all-purpose potatoes, peeled

1 large carrot, peeled

1 teaspoon salt

80 ml (2½ fl oz/⅓ cup) vegetable oil

6 eggs

SERVES 6

1 Coarsely grate the potatoes and carrot. Place in a colander, sprinkle over the salt. Stand for 10 minutes.

2 Use your hands to squeeze out as much moisture from the potato mixture as possible.

3 Heat 3 tablespoons of the oil in a large frying pan over medium–high heat. Add ¾ cup of the potato mixture to the pan, shaping it into a patty with a 10 cm (4 inch) diameter. Repeat with another ¾ cup of the mixture. Cook for 5 minutes, or until golden underneath. Turn the röstis over and cook for a further 5 minutes or until crisp, golden and cooked through. Remove from the pan, set aside and keep warm. Repeat with the remaining mixture to make six röstis in total.

4 Just before serving, heat the remaining 1 tablespoon oil in a separate frying pan over medium–high heat and crack the eggs in separately (you may have to cook them in batches). Cook for 2 minutes.

5 Serve each rösti topped with a fried egg and sprinkled with a little salt and black pepper, if desired.

# scottish pancakes

**SCOTLAND** Sometimes referred to as drop scones, these pancakes are slightly smaller and a bit thicker than American pancakes. Scottish pancakes are often served for breakfast or morning tea with butter and jam — breakfast doesn't get much tastier than this!

110 g (3¾ oz/¾ cup) plain (all-purpose) flour

1 teaspoon baking powder

150 ml (5 fl oz) buttermilk, at room temperature

1 egg

1 tablespoon vegetable oil

1 tablespoon golden syrup

60 g (2¼ oz/½ cup) sultanas (golden raisins)

butter, for greasing

MAKES 8

1 Sift the flour and baking powder into a large bowl and make a well in the centre.

2 In a separate bowl, whisk together the buttermilk, egg, oil and golden syrup. Add to the flour mixture and stir with a whisk until smooth. Add the sultanas and gently fold through using a large metal spoon or spatula.

3 Heat a little butter in a frying pan over medium heat, swirling to coat the base of the pan. Add a heaped tablespoon of pancake batter to the pan for each pancake — you will need to do this in batches and not crowd the pan. Cook for about 2 minutes, or until bubbles appear on the surface of the pancakes. Flip them over and cook for another 2 minutes, or until golden underneath and cooked through. Transfer to a plate, cover with foil to keep warm and repeat with the remaining batter.

4 Serve the warm pancakes with butter and jam.

# french toast

**FRANCE** Known as *pain perdu* in France, this dish was traditionally made using stale bread, dipped in a mixture of egg and milk, sweetened with vanilla and fried to make a delicious dessert. In other parts of the world it is eaten for breakfast!

4 eggs, lightly beaten

200 ml (7 fl oz) milk

1 teaspoon natural vanilla extract

1 tablespoon icing (confectioners') sugar, sifted

½ teaspoon ground cinnamon

¼ teaspoon ground nutmeg

4 x 2 cm (¾ inch) slices day-old white sourdough bread or brioche

40 g (1½ oz) butter

2 ripe bananas, sliced lengthways, to serve

maple syrup, to serve

icing (confectioners') sugar, to serve (optional)

**SERVES 4**

1  Preheat the oven to 120°C (235°F/Gas ½). Combine the egg, milk, vanilla, icing sugar, cinnamon and nutmeg in a large bowl and whisk with a fork until well combined.

2  Dip two of the bread slices into the milk mixture for 1 minute until well soaked.

3  Heat half of the butter in a large frying pan over medium heat. Remove the bread slices from the egg mixture and allow any excess to drain off. Add the soaked bread to the pan and cook for 1–2 minutes each side, or until golden. Transfer to a baking tray and place in the oven to keep warm. Repeat with the remaining bread, egg mixture and butter.

4  Place the French toast onto plates and serve topped with banana slices and maple syrup, and sprinkled with icing sugar, if desired.

# swiss creamed baked eggs

**SWITZERLAND** Swiss cuisine was originally influenced by its farmers, who were famous for producing quality cheeses and cream. This dish is a quick and simple breakfast that uses these ingredients — we have added spinach to give it a little freshness.

100 g (3½ oz/2 cups) baby spinach, washed, dried and stems trimmed

butter, for greasing

40 g (1½ oz/⅓ cup) coarsely grated Gruyère cheese

80 ml (2½ fl oz/⅓ cup) pouring (whipping) cream

4 eggs

SERVES 4

1   Preheat the oven to 180°C (350°C/Gas 4). Put the spinach in a large bowl and cover with boiling water. Stand for 30 seconds. Drain and rinse under cold water. Use your hands to squeeze out as much liquid as possible.

2   Grease four 125 ml (4 fl oz/½ cup) ovenproof dishes with butter and place on a baking tray. Divide the spinach among the dishes. Season with salt and black pepper and sprinkle with half of the cheese.

3   Make a well in the centre of the cheese and spinach in each dish — this will be for the egg to sit in. Break an egg into each well, then divide the cream evenly over the tops and sprinkle with the remaining cheese.

4   Bake for 8–10 minutes, or until the egg white has set but the yolk is still soft.

5   Carefully place the dishes onto a serving plate and serve immediately with buttered toast on the side.

# sweet couscous

MOROCCO  Couscous is a popular North African cereal made from semolina flour. It is often eaten with savoury dishes instead of rice, but in Morocco and Egypt it is also sweetened with dried fruits and nuts, making it a tasty and healthy dish to start the day.

80 g (2¾ oz/½ cup) combined pistachio nuts, pine nuts and blanched almonds

45 g (1¾ oz/¼ cup) dried apricots

90 g (3¼ oz/½ cup) dried pitted dates

250 g (9 oz/1⅓ cups) instant couscous

250 ml (9 fl oz/1 cup) boiling water

2 tablespoons honey

50 g (1¾ oz) unsalted butter, softened

2 tablespoons caster (superfine) sugar

½ teaspoon ground cinnamon

SERVES 4–6

1  Preheat the oven to 160°C (315°F/Gas 2–3). Spread the nuts on a baking tray and cook for 5–8 minutes, or until light golden. Allow to cool, then chop them coarsely and place in a bowl.

2  Meanwhile, slice the apricots into matchstick-sized pieces and quarter the dates lengthways. Add both to the bowl with the nuts and toss to combine.

3  Put the couscous in a large, heatproof bowl. Combine the boiling water, honey and butter in a separate bowl and stir well. Add to the couscous and stir until the butter melts completely. Cover with a tea towel (dish towel) and set aside for 5 minutes. Fluff the couscous with a fork to separate the grains, then toss in half of the fruit and nut mixture (see note).

4  To serve, spoon the warm couscous into serving bowls. Sprinkle with the remaining fruit and nut mixture. Combine the sugar and cinnamon in a small bowl and sprinkle over the couscous. Serve with hot milk.

**Note:** The couscous can be made up to 2 days ahead. Store in an airtight container in the refrigerator. To reheat, bring to room temperature, transfer to an ovenproof dish, cover with foil and reheat in a preheated 180°C (350°F/Gas 4) oven for 20 minutes.

# californian smoothies

USA  In the 1930s health food shops in the United States began selling puréed fruit drinks, made with fruit, fruit juice and ice. Known as 'smoothies' they are now often made with milk or yoghurt.

## tropical smoothie

2 bananas, peeled and sliced

½ mango, peeled and chopped

250 ml (9 fl oz/1 cup) milk

1 teaspoon natural vanilla extract

2 teaspoons honey, or to taste

1 passionfruit, pulp removed

SERVES 2

1  Place all of the ingredients, except the passionfruit pulp, into a blender and blend until smooth and creamy. Pour into glasses and stir in the passionfruit pulp. Serve immediately.

## thick berry smoothie

250 g (9 oz/2 cups) frozen mixed berries

250 ml (9 fl oz/1 cup) milk

200 g (7 oz) berry-flavoured yoghurt

1½ tablespoons sugar, or to taste

SERVES 2

1  Remove the frozen berries from the freezer and allow them to thaw for 5 minutes (don't thaw them completely).

2  Place all of the ingredients into a blender and purée until smooth. Pour into glasses and serve immediately.

## strawberry yoghurt smoothie

150 g (5½ oz/1 cup) strawberries, hulled and halved

250 g (9 oz/1 cup) vanilla yoghurt

125 ml (4 fl oz/½ cup) cranberry juice

60 ml (2 fl oz/¼ cup) orange juice

honey, to taste

SERVES 2

1  Place all of the ingredients into a blender and blend until smooth and creamy. Pour into glasses and serve immediately.

## peanut butter and banana smoothie

500 ml (17 fl oz/2 cups) milk

1 tablespoon smooth peanut butter

1 ripe banana, sliced

2 teaspoons honey, or to taste

1 cup ice cubes

SERVES 2

1  Place all of the ingredients into a blender and process until the mixture is smooth and creamy. Pour into glasses and serve immediately.

# lunchtime and snacks

# nachos

MEXICO This tasty dish originated in Mexico where it was made with pieces of tortilla, a type of fried flat bread. This snack is now often made with corn chips.

440 g (15½ oz/2 cups) tin red kidney beans

2 tablespoons vegetable oil

1 large onion, finely chopped

2 garlic cloves, crushed

2 large ripe tomatoes, chopped

125 g (4½ oz/½ cup) bottled tomato salsa

Tabasco sauce (optional), to taste

175 g (6 oz) pkt corn chips

250 g (9 oz/2 cups) grated cheddar cheese

guacamole (see below) and sour cream, to serve

SERVES 6

1 Preheat the oven to 180°C (350°F/Gas 4). Rinse the kidney beans in a colander, drain well and roughly mash with a fork.

2 Heat the oil in a frying pan over medium heat and cook the onion and garlic for 4–5 minutes, or until softened.

3 Add the tomato, tomato salsa and mashed kidney beans and cook over medium heat for 5 minutes, or until the tomato softens. Season to taste with the Tabasco sauce, if using.

4 Arrange half of the corn chips in a large shallow ovenproof dish. Top with half of the kidney bean mixture and half of the cheese. Repeat with the remaining ingredients to make a second layer (leave some of the corn chips showing if possible). Cook in the oven for 10–15 minutes, or until the cheese has melted and the nachos are heated through. Serve the nachos with guacamole and sour cream.

# guacamole

MEXICO The word guacamole is most likely derived from the words *ahuacti*, meaning 'avocado' and *molli*, meaning 'sauce'. It is often served as a dip or alongside nachos.

2 ripe avocados

½ small red onion, finely chopped

1 ripe tomato, diced

1 tablespoon chopped fresh coriander (cilantro) leaves

1 tablespoon freshly squeezed lemon juice

SERVES 6

1 Cut the avocados in half and remove the stones.

2 Peel the avocados and place the flesh into a bowl. Mash with a fork until almost smooth.

3 Add the onion, tomato, coriander and lemon juice. Stir to combine. Serve with nachos (see above) or as a dip with pitta bread, vegetable sticks or corn chips.

# thai fish cakes

**THAILAND**  These popular fish cakes make a terrific lunch or snack and use some of the more popular flavourings of Thai cookery, including lemongrass and coriander.

500 g (1 lb 2 oz) boneless white fish fillets, chopped

1 lemongrass stem, pale part only, chopped

2 tablespoons fish sauce

5 spring onions (scallions), chopped

3 tablespoons chopped coriander (cilantro)

1 garlic clove, crushed

150 ml (5 fl oz) tin coconut milk

1 tablespoon sweet chilli sauce

1 egg

60 g (2¼ oz) green beans, thinly sliced

80 ml (2½ fl oz/⅓ cup) peanut oil

**sauce**

90 g (3¼ oz) sugar

2 tablespoons sweet chilli sauce

½ small Lebanese (short) cucumber, diced

MAKES 28

1  Place the fish, lemongrass, fish sauce, spring onion, coriander, garlic, coconut milk, sweet chilli sauce and egg in a food processor and process until smooth. Transfer to a bowl and mix in the beans. With wet hands, shape tablespoonfuls of the mixture into patties. Place on a plate, cover with plastic wrap and refrigerate for 30 minutes for them to firm up.

2  To make the sauce, put the sugar in a small saucepan with 80 ml (2½ fl oz/⅓ cup) water. Cook over low heat for 2 minutes, or until the sugar has dissolved. Increase the heat and simmer for 5 minutes, or until slightly thickened. Remove from the heat and stir in the sweet chilli sauce. Cool and stir in the diced cucumber.

3  Heat the oil in a large heavy-based frying pan over medium heat. Cook the fish cakes, in batches, for 2 minutes on each side, or until cooked through. Serve the warm fish cakes with the sauce on the side for dipping.

# san choy bao

**CHINA** Translating as 'lettuce delights', *san choy bao* is a popular pork mince dish served as part of larger banquets and on its own makes a great light lunch. Instead of using a knife and fork, you can pick up the lettuce cups and munch on them like a burger.

1 tablespoon peanut oil

1 teaspoon sesame oil

1–2 garlic cloves, crushed

1 tablespoon finely grated fresh ginger

4 spring onions (scallions), chopped

500 g (1 lb 2 oz) minced (ground) pork

1 red capsicum (pepper), seeded, membrane removed and diced

220 g (7¾ oz) tin water chestnuts, drained and roughly chopped

1–2 tablespoons soy sauce

1 tablespoon oyster sauce

2 tablespoons chicken stock

4 iceberg lettuce leaves

**SERVES 4**

1 Heat the peanut and sesame oils in a large, non-stick frying pan or wok over medium heat. Add the garlic, ginger and spring onion and stir-fry for 2 minutes. Add the pork and cook until well browned, breaking up any lumps with a fork or wooden spoon.

2 Stir in the capsicum, water chestnuts, soy and oyster sauces and stock. Simmer over medium heat until the liquid reduces and thickens. Keep warm.

3 Use a pair of kitchen scissors to trim the edges of the lettuce leaves to make neat cup shapes and place in bowls or on a plate. Spoon the pork filling into the lettuce leaves and serve.

# indian lamb wraps

**INDIA** Indian food is known for its use of many fragrant spices, herbs and flavourings. Another big part of Indian cooking is rice or bread (chapati), yoghurts and chutneys. This recipe is not a traditional dish as such, instead it borrows some of the key elements of the cuisine.

500 g (1 lb 2 oz) minced (ground) lamb

1 small brown onion, finely diced

1 garlic clove, crushed

1 tablespoon garam masala

¼ cup chopped mint leaves

1½ tablespoons mango chutney

1 egg, lightly beaten

60 ml (2 fl oz/¼ cup) canola oil

8 chapati breads, warmed following packet directions

50 g (1¾ oz/1 cup) baby spinach leaves

1 Lebanese (short) cucumber, cut into batons

1 carrot, peeled and finely shredded

2 ripe tomatoes, cut into wedges

plain yoghurt or extra mango chutney, to serve

SERVES 4

1 Combine the lamb, onion, garlic, garam masala, mint, chutney and egg in a bowl; season with salt and black pepper. Use your hands to mix until combined. Shape the mixture into 16 patties, about 6 cm (2½ inches) in diameter and 2 cm (¾ inch) thick. Place on a tray and refrigerate for 15 minutes.

2 Heat the oil in a large frying pan over medium–high heat. Cook the patties for 5 minutes on each side, or until browned and cooked through — do this in two batches.

3 Top each chapati with some spinach, cucumber, carrot, tomato and a lamb patty. Top with a dollop of chutney or yoghurt and roll up to enclose the filling.

# falafel

**LEBANON** This delicious snack is also made in many other Middle Eastern countries and is a popular street food, often sold wrapped in pitta bread with hummus, tahini sauce and salad.

220 g (7¾ oz/1 cup) dried chickpeas

1 brown onion, chopped

6 garlic cloves, chopped

2 teaspoons ground coriander

1 tablespoon ground cumin

¼ teaspoon chilli powder

½ teaspoon bicarbonate of soda (baking soda)

½ cup chopped flat-leaf (Italian) parsley leaves

3 tablespoons chopped coriander (cilantro) leaves

170 ml (5½ fl oz/⅔ cup) vegetable oil

**MAKES ABOUT 30**

1  Place the chickpeas in a large bowl, cover with water and soak for 12 hours or overnight.

2  Drain the chickpeas well, then process in a food processor with the onion and garlic until smooth. Add the ground coriander, cumin, chilli powder, bicarbonate of soda and fresh herbs. Season with salt and black pepper, to taste, and process until well combined.

3  Shape tablespoons of the mixture into patties about 1 cm (½ inch) thick, place on a tray, and refrigerate for at least 20 minutes before cooking.

4  Heat the oil in a deep frying pan over medium–high heat. Cook the falafels, in batches, for 2 minutes each side or until golden. Drain on paper towels. Serve warm or cold with hummus (see below) and pitta bread.

# hummus (chickpea dip)

**LEBANON** This popular dip can be served with just about anything, although traditionally it is served with black olives and pitta bread.

400 g (14 oz) tin chickpeas

1 tablespoon tahini

2 garlic cloves, crushed

1 teaspoon ground cumin

2 tablespoons freshly squeezed lemon juice

1½ tablespoons olive oil

1 small pinch of cayenne pepper

½ teaspoon salt

chopped flat-leaf (Italian) parsley, to serve

**MAKES 1½ CUPS**

1  Rinse the chickpeas and drain well.

2  Place the chickpeas, tahini, garlic, cumin, lemon juice, oil, cayenne pepper and salt in a food processor and process until thick and smooth. With the motor running, gradually add 60 ml (2 fl oz/¼ cup) water, to form a creamy purée. Season with a little more salt or some extra lemon juice, if desired.

3  Spoon the hummus into a serving dish, drizzle with a little extra oil, sprinkle with a little extra cayenne pepper and garnish with the parsley. Serve with falafels (see above) and pitta bread or as a dip.

# cornish pasties

**ENGLAND** These tempting pasties might sound like they are filled with corn, but really they originated in the English county of Cornwall. They had meat in one end and jam in the other, making lunch and dessert for Cornish tin miners. So robust were the pasties that it was believed you could drop one down a mine shaft and it wouldn't break!

4 sheets frozen shortcrust pastry, thawed

1 egg, lightly beaten

**filling**

160 g (5¾ oz) trimmed rump steak, finely chopped

1 small potato, finely chopped

1 small brown onion, finely chopped

1 small carrot, finely chopped

2 teaspoons Worcestershire sauce

2 tablespoons beef stock

MAKES 8

1  Line a large baking tray with baking paper. Preheat the oven to 210°C (415°F/Gas 6–7).

2  To make the filling, mix together the steak, potato, onion, carrot, Worcestershire sauce and stock in a bowl and season with salt and black pepper.

3  Using a plate with a 14 cm (5½ inch) diameter as a guide, cut two rounds from each sheet of pastry. Divide the filling among the rounds. Brush the edges lightly with the egg and bring the pastry together to enclose the filling, pinching the edges together to seal. Place on the prepared tray and brush each pasty lightly with a little more egg.

4  Bake the pasties in the oven for 15–20 minutes, or until cooked through and golden. Serve warm.

# arancini

**ITALY** Arancini means 'little oranges', referring to their shape, colour and size. A speciality of Sicily they are made of rice and saffron wrapped around a filling, then dipped in breadcrumbs and fried. This recipe uses a cheese filling and the balls are flattened slightly for easy cooking.

1 litre (35 fl oz/4 cups) chicken stock

1 large pinch of saffron threads

100 g (3½ oz) butter

1 brown onion, finely chopped

1 garlic clove, crushed

2 tablespoons thyme leaves

220 g (7¾ oz/1 cup) arborio rice

50 g (1¾ oz/½ cup) grated parmesan cheese

80 g (2¾ oz) fresh mozzarella or fontina cheese, cut into 1 cm (½ inch) cubes

80 g (2¾ oz/¾ cup) dry breadcrumbs

250 ml (9 fl oz/1 cup) olive oil

**MAKES ABOUT 40**

1 Put the stock into a saucepan and bring to the boil. Add the saffron, cover, reduce the heat and keep the stock at a gentle simmer.

2 Melt the butter in a large saucepan over medium heat and cook the onion and garlic for 5 minutes, or until softened. Add the thyme and rice and cook, stirring, for 1 minute, or until the rice is well coated. Add about 125 ml (4 fl oz/½ cup) of the hot stock to the pan and stir constantly until all the liquid is absorbed. Continue adding more stock, ½ cup at a time, until all the liquid is absorbed and the rice is tender and creamy; this will take about 25–30 minutes.

3 Cover a tray with plastic wrap. Remove the pan from the heat and stir in the parmesan. Spread the mixture out onto the tray. Set aside to cool and, for the best results, cover and leave in the refrigerator overnight.

4 Roll a tablespoonful of the risotto into a ball. Press a hole in the middle with your thumb, push a cube of mozzarella cheese inside and press the risotto around it to enclose in a ball. Flatten the ball slightly into a patty, about 1.5 cm (⅝ inch) thick. Repeat with the rest of the risotto. Roll each patty in the breadcrumbs to coat both sides.

5 Heat the oil in a deep frying pan over high heat until hot. Cook the arancini in batches, without crowding, for 2 minutes each side, or until golden brown. Drain on paper towels and leave to cool down slightly. Serve warm with lemon wedges on the side.

# dolmades (stuffed vine leaves)

**GREECE**  It is thought that the first dolmades were eaten during the time of Alexander the Great. During this time warring armies had little food to eat and would wrap small morsels of meat and rice in vine leaves to eat. Since then the recipe has been perfected to make this tasty snack.

200 g (7 oz) marinated vine leaves

220 g (7¾ oz/1 cup) short-grain white rice

1 small brown onion, finely chopped

100 ml (3½ fl oz) olive oil

60 g (2¼ oz) pine nuts, toasted

2 tablespoons currants

2 tablespoons chopped dill

1 tablespoon finely chopped mint leaves

1 tablespoon finely chopped flat-leaf (Italian) parsley leaves

2 tablespoons freshly squeezed lemon juice

500 ml (17 fl oz/2 cups) chicken stock

lemon wedges, to serve

MAKES 24

1  Soak the vine leaves in cold water for 15 minutes, then remove and pat dry. Cut off any stems. Reserve some leaves to line the saucepan and discard any that have holes. Meanwhile, place the rice in a large heatproof bowl and pour over boiling water. Set aside to soak for 10 minutes. Drain well.

2  Place the rice, onion, 1 tablespoon of the olive oil, pine nuts, currants and herbs in a bowl and season with salt and black pepper. Mix well to combine.

3  Lay some vine leaves, vein side down, on a flat surface. Place 1 tablespoon of the rice filling in the centre of each, fold the stalk end over the filling, then the left and right sides into the centre, and finally roll firmly towards the tip. Repeat with the remaining filling and leaves to make about 24 dolmades.

4  Use the remaining vine leaves to line the base of a large heavy-based saucepan. Drizzle the leaves with 1 tablespoon of the oil. Add the dolmades, packing them tightly in one layer. Pour the remaining oil and the lemon juice over the top.

5  Pour the stock over the dolmades and cover with an inverted plate to stop the dolmades moving around while cooking. Bring to the boil, then reduce the heat to low, cover, and simmer for 45 minutes, or until the filling is cooked. Remove the dolmades from the saucepan with a slotted spoon. Serve warm or cold with lemon wedges.

# börek (lamb filo fingers)

**TURKEY** These thin flaky pastries are most often filled with a mixture of cheese, minced meat and vegetables. Lamb filo fingers are a popular version of this classic dish and are traditionally served as a snack with Turkish tea.

1 tablespoon olive oil

350 g (12 oz) minced (ground) lamb

1 small brown onion, finely chopped

2 garlic cloves, crushed

1 tablespoon ground cumin

1 teaspoon ground ginger

1 teaspoon paprika

1 teaspoon ground cinnamon

¼ teaspoon chilli flakes

2 tablespoons chopped coriander (cilantro) leaves

2 tablespoons chopped flat-leaf (Italian) parsley leaves

3 tablespoons pine nuts, toasted

1 egg

16 sheets filo pastry

100 g (3½ oz) butter, melted

1 tablespoon sesame seeds

### yoghurt sauce

250 g (9 oz/1 cup) plain yoghurt

2 tablespoons chopped mint leaves

1 garlic clove, crushed

MAKES 16

1 Preheat the oven to 180°C (350°F/Gas 4). Lightly grease a large baking tray.

2 Heat the oil in a large frying pan over medium–high heat and cook the lamb for 5 minutes, breaking up any lumps with a wooden spoon. Add the onion and garlic and cook for 1 minute. Add the spices, coriander and parsley and cook, stirring to combine, for 1 minute or until fragrant. Transfer the mixture to a sieve and drain to remove the fat.

3 Place the mixture in a bowl and cool slightly. Mix in the pine nuts and egg until well combined.

4 Lay the filo pastry sheets flat on a kitchen bench, cover with a dry tea towel (dish towel) and then a slightly damp one to prevent them from drying out. Take a sheet of filo and place on the bench with the shortest side facing you. Brush with melted butter and then fold in half lengthways. Place 1 tablespoon of the lamb mixture at the end of the strip and roll up, tucking in the ends to hold the mixture in, to form each into a finger shape. Place on the baking tray. Repeat with the remaining filo and meat to make 16 fingers in total

5 Brush the fingers with any remaining melted butter and sprinkle with the sesame seeds. Bake for 15 minutes, or until lightly golden and crisp.

6 Meanwhile, to make the yoghurt sauce, stir all the ingredients together in a small bowl. Serve the filo fingers warm with the yoghurt sauce for dipping.

# vietnamese fresh spring rolls

**VIETNAM** Vietnamese cuisine has been influenced by the Chinese who dominated the region for almost 1000 years and the French who were a colonial power for 100 years. These spring rolls are served cold and use vermicelli noodles and rice wrappers — both traditional staples.

12 cooked king prawns (shrimp)

12 x 21 cm (8¼ inch) rice paper rounds

50 g (1¾ oz) rice vermicelli, soaked in hot water for 5 minutes then drained well

¼ iceberg lettuce, finely shredded

2 small carrots, coarsely grated

90 g (3¼ oz/1 cup) bean sprouts, trimmed

1 Lebanese (short) cucumber, peeled, seeded and cut into thin batons

24 mint leaves

½ cup coriander (cilantro) leaves

hoisin sauce or sweet chilli sauce, for dipping

MAKES 12

1 Peel the prawns, remove the heads and devein. Cut in half lengthways.

2 Half-fill a bowl with warm water. One at a time, place a rice paper round into the water for 15–20 seconds, until it starts to soften (the time will depend on the brand of the wrappers and the heat of the water). Remove from the water and lay on a clean tea towel (dish towel).

3 Lay some cold vermicelli at one end of the rice paper, leaving a 2 cm (¾ inch) border at both ends. Top with some lettuce, carrot, bean sprouts and cucumber. Roll halfway and fold both sides over to enclose the filling. Place 2 prawn halves, cut side down, on top of the roll, top with some mint and coriander and roll tightly to enclose the filling completely. Place on a plate and cover with damp paper towels. Repeat with the remaining rice paper rounds and filling ingredients.

4 Arrange the rolls on a plate and serve with the sauces on the side for dipping.

# risi e bisi (pea and rice soup)

**ITALY** Literally translating as 'rice and peas' in Italian, this popular dish is often served in spring time when peas are at their seasonal best. It should always be served with a spoon — its consistency should resemble a thick soup or a very wet risotto.

1.5 litres (52 fl oz/6 cups) chicken or vegetable stock

2 teaspoons olive oil

40 g (1½ oz) unsalted butter

1 small brown onion, finely chopped

80 g (2¾ oz) pancetta, finely chopped

375 g (13 oz) fresh or frozen peas

2 tablespoons chopped flat-leaf (Italian) parsley

220 g (7¾ oz/1 cup) arborio rice

50 g (1¾ oz/½ cup) finely grated parmesan cheese

**SERVES 4–6**

1 Put the stock in a saucepan over medium heat and bring to the boil. Reduce the heat, cover and keep at a gentle simmer.

2 Heat the oil and half the butter in a large heavy-based saucepan over medium heat. Add the onion and pancetta and cook for 5 minutes, or until the onion has softened.

3 Stir in the peas and parsley and add 500 ml (17 fl oz/2 cups) of the stock. Simmer for about 6–8 minutes, stirring well.

4 Add the rice and the remaining stock and cook gently for 12–15 minutes, stirring occasionally, or until the rice is *al dente*.

5 Stir in the parmesan and remaining butter, season with salt and black pepper and serve immediately.

# corn chowder

USA  A chowder usually refers to any kind of soup that has been thickened with flour or milk. This corn chowder is reminiscent of clam and fish chowders that were popular with colonial settlers in the United States. Today there is hot debate about the best way to make a chowder.

90 g (3¼ oz) unsalted butter

2 large brown onions, finely chopped

1 garlic clove, crushed

2 teaspoons cumin seeds

1 litre (35 fl oz/4 cups) vegetable stock

2 potatoes, peeled and chopped

250 g (9 oz/1 cup) tin creamed corn

400 g (14 oz/2 cups) fresh corn kernels
(about 4 cobs)

¼ cup chopped flat-leaf (Italian) parsley

125 g (4½ oz/1 cup) grated cheddar cheese

3 tablespoons pouring (whipping) cream (optional)

2 tablespoons snipped chives (optional), to serve

SERVES 8

1   Melt the butter in a large heavy-based saucepan over medium–high heat. Add the onion and cook for 5 minutes, or until golden.

2   Add the garlic and cumin and cook for 1 minute, stirring constantly, then pour in the stock and bring to the boil. Add the potato, then reduce the heat and simmer for 10 minutes.

3   Add the creamed corn, corn kernels and parsley to the pan. Bring to the boil, then reduce the heat and simmer for 10 minutes.

4   Stir in the cheese and season to taste with salt and black pepper. Stir in the cream, if using, and heat gently until the cheese melts. Serve immediately, sprinkled with the chives if desired.

# thai noodle salad

**THAILAND** Thai cuisine is a mixture of sweet and sour, salty and spicy flavours and has been influenced by surrounding countries such as China and India. Like many Asian countries, Thai food uses lots of rice and noodles, and fresh herbs, spices, ginger and a variety of Asian sauces.

200 g (7 oz) mung bean vermicelli noodles

5 spring onions (scallions), sliced

1 red capsicum (pepper), seeded, membrane removed and cut into thin strips

100 g (3½ oz/1 cup) snow peas (mangetout), sliced

500 g (1 lb 2 oz) cooked king prawns (shrimp), peeled, halved lengthways and deveined

¼ cup coriander (cilantro) leaves

**dressing**

2 tablespoons finely grated fresh ginger

1½ tablespoons soy sauce

2 teaspoons sesame oil

2 tablespoons rice wine vinegar

3–4 teaspoons sweet chilli sauce

2 garlic cloves, crushed

60 ml (2 fl oz/¼ cup) kecap manis

2 tablespoons freshly squeezed lime juice

SERVES 4

1   To make the dressing, put the ingredients in a large bowl and whisk with a fork to combine.

2   Place the noodles in a large bowl and cover with warm water. Stand for 5 minutes, or until tender. Drain well, then add to the bowl with the dressing and toss to combine and coat the noodles.

3   Add the spring onion, capsicum, snow peas, prawns and coriander and toss gently. Serve the salad at room temperature.

# seekh kebabs

**PAKISTAN**  A seekh kebab is a Pakistani version of beef cooked on skewers. One story has it that they were invented by soldiers who used their swords to grill meat over open campfires.

pinch of ground cloves

pinch of ground nutmeg

½ teaspoon chilli powder

1 teaspoon ground cumin

2 teaspoons ground coriander

3 garlic cloves, finely chopped

5 cm (2 inch) piece fresh ginger, finely grated

500 g (1 lb 2 oz) minced (ground) beef

1 tablespoon olive oil

2 tablespoons freshly squeezed lemon juice

**onion and mint relish**

1 red onion, finely chopped

1 tablespoon white vinegar

1 tablespoon freshly squeezed lemon juice

1 tablespoon chopped mint leaves

SERVES 4

1  Soak 12 wooden skewers in cold water for 30 minutes to prevent them from burning during cooking.

2  Dry-fry the cloves, nutmeg, chilli, cumin and coriander in a heavy-based frying pan over low heat for about 2 minutes, shaking the pan constantly. Transfer to a bowl with the garlic and ginger and set aside.

3  Use your hands to knead the beef constantly for about 3 minutes, or until it becomes very soft and a little sticky — this process changes the texture of the meat when cooked, making it very soft and tender. Add the spice, garlic and ginger mixture and mix thoroughly, seasoning well with salt and black pepper.

4  Shape tablespoons of the meat into small balls. Wet your hands and press three balls of the meat onto each skewer, leaving a gap of about 1 cm (½ inch) between each and pressing each into an oval shape. Repeat with the remaining meat to make 12 kebabs.

5  To make the onion and mint relish, mix together the onion, vinegar and lemon juice and refrigerate for 10 minutes. Stir in the mint and season with black pepper just before serving.

6  Preheat an oiled barbecue grill or chargrill pan to high and cook the kebabs for about 8 minutes, turning regularly and sprinkling with a little lemon juice, or until cooked through. Serve with the onion and mint relish and a shredded carrot salad.

# thai beef salad

**THAILAND**  One of the best things about Thai food is that it is simple to cook and tastes terrific. This beef salad makes a great lunch and uses some of the classic Thai flavourings, such as coriander and garlic, to marinate the meat before cooking.

3 garlic cloves, finely chopped

4 coriander (cilantro) roots, finely chopped

½ teaspoon black pepper

60 ml (2 fl oz/¼ cup) peanut oil

400 g (14 oz) rump or sirloin steak

1 small oakleaf lettuce, leaves separated

200 g (7 oz) cherry tomatoes, halved

1 Lebanese (short) cucumber, halved lengthways and sliced

4 spring onions (scallions), sliced

1 large handful coriander (cilantro) leaves

**dressing**

1½ tablespoons fish sauce

2 tablespoons freshly squeezed lime juice

1 tablespoon soy sauce

½ fresh long red chilli, seeded and finely chopped

2 teaspoons soft brown sugar or finely grated palm sugar (jaggery)

SERVES 4

1  Finely grind the garlic, coriander roots, pepper and 2 tablespoons of the oil using a mortar and pestle, food processor or blender to make a chunky paste. Spread evenly over both sides of the steak.

2  Heat the remaining oil in a heavy-based frying pan or chargrill pan over high heat. Cook the steak for about 4 minutes on each side, turning once, for medium or until cooked to your liking (see note). Set aside to cool.

3  Meanwhile, combine the lettuce, cherry tomato halves, cucumber and spring onion in a large bowl.

4  To make the dressing, stir together all the ingredients until the sugar has dissolved.

5  Cut the steak into thin strips. Add to the bowl with the salad and toss together very gently. Drizzle with the dressing and scatter the coriander leaves over the top. Serve immediately.

**Note:** Be careful that you don't overcook the steak — it should be pink and, therefore, succulent and tender.

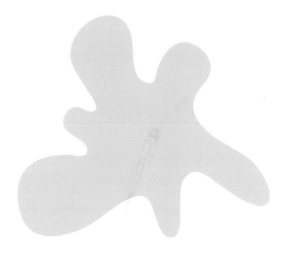

# quiche lorraine

**FRANCE** There are many different kinds of quiches and all resemble an open pie using eggs and cream in a light pastry with various flavourings added. This quiche recipe is particular to the Lorraine region of France and traditionally includes bacon and cheese.

2 sheets frozen shortcrust pastry, thawed

30 g (1 oz) butter

1 brown onion, finely chopped

4 bacon slices, finely chopped

120 g (4¼ oz/1 cup) grated Gruyère cheese

4 eggs

350 ml (12 fl oz) pouring (whipping) cream

½ teaspoon ground nutmeg

2 tablespoons snipped chives

**SERVES 4**

1 Lightly grease four 12 cm (4½ inch) fluted flan (tart) tins with removable bases. Line the tins with the pastry, easing it gently into the base and side; trim the edges. Place the tins on a baking tray and freeze the pastry for 30 minutes, or until frozen.

2 Preheat the oven to 190°C (375°F/Gas 5). Cook the frozen pastry cases for 15 minutes, or until the pastry is just cooked but still pale.

3 Meanwhile, to make the filling, melt the butter in a small frying pan and cook the onion and bacon over medium heat for 5 minutes, or until the onion softens. Drain on paper towels. Divide the mixture among the warm pastry cases. Sprinkle over the cheese.

4 In a jug, gently whisk together the eggs and cream and season with salt, black pepper and the nutmeg. Divide evenly among the pastry cases over the bacon mixture and sprinkle with the chives. Bake on the tray for 20 minutes, or until the filling is just set. Leave in the tins for 5 minutes before removing carefully and serving with a green salad.

# sushi rolls

**JAPAN** Sushi is the Japanese word to describe any type of cooked vinegared rice, topped with a variety of different ingredients, from fish to chicken, vegetables and tofu, and rolled inside preserved sheets of dried seaweed, called *nori*.

1 Lebanese (short) cucumber

3 sheets nori (dried seaweed)

½ firm ripe avocado, thinly sliced

185 g (6½ oz) tin tuna in springwater

30 g (1 oz) pickled ginger (optional)

125 g (4½ oz/½ cup) mayonnaise

1–2 teaspoons wasabi paste (optional)

2 teaspoons soy sauce

**sushi rice**

260 g (9¼ oz/1¼ cups) sushi rice

60 ml (2 fl oz/¼ cup) rice vinegar

1 tablespoon caster (superfine) sugar

1 teaspoon salt

MAKES 18

1 To make the sushi rice, put the rice and 435 ml (15¼ fl oz/1¾ cups) water in a saucepan with a tight-fitting lid and bring to the boil. Reduce the heat to low and cook for 12–15 minutes, or until all the water is absorbed. Set aside, covered, for 10 minutes.

2 Place the vinegar, sugar and salt in a small saucepan and stir over low heat until the sugar and salt dissolve.

3 Transfer the rice to a large non-metallic dish and sprinkle with the seasoned rice vinegar. Use a large spatula or spoon to gently fold the vinegar evenly through the rice. Set aside, uncovered, for 30 minutes, or until cooled to room temperature.

4 When you are ready to make the sushi rolls, halve the cucumber lengthways and remove the seeds with a teaspoon. Cut each length into 4 wedges.

5 Lay a nori sheet, shiny side down, on a bamboo sushi mat (with the slats running horizontally). Use damp hands to spread one-third of the rice over the nori leaving a 2 cm (¾ inch) border at the far end. Arrange a third of the cucumber, avocado, tuna and ginger, if using, lengthways over the rice, about one-third of the way up from the bottom edge. Combine the mayonnaise, wasabi and soy sauce and spread a little over the top.

6 Use your thumbs and forefingers to hold the fillings in place while lifting the mat over to enclose. Continue to roll the nori and fillings, using the mat to gently pull and tighten into a neat log. Unroll the mat and wrap the sushi tightly in plastic wrap. Repeat to make two more rolls.

7 To serve, trim the ends of the rolls with a sharp knife and then cut each into six slices. Serve with the remaining wasabi mayonnaise mixture.

# enchiladas

**MEXICO**  The enchilada is one of the most popular dishes sold in Mexico. The term enchilada simply means 'dipped in chilli'. Traditionally it was made with a corn tortilla folded around small fish. This recipe is based on *Enchiladas Suizas* (Swiss) which means it uses cheese and cream.

2 tablespoons olive oil

1 brown onion, finely diced

1 red capsicum, seeded, membrane removed and finely diced

2 garlic cloves, crushed

1 kg (2 lb 4 oz) minced (ground) beef

2 tablespoons ground cumin

1 tablespoon sweet paprika

½ teaspoon chilli flakes

100 g (3½ oz/⅓ cup) tomato paste (concentrated purée)

400 g (14 oz/1⅔ cups) tin chopped tomatoes

400 g (14 oz/2 cups) tin red kidney beans, rinsed and drained

12 x 25 cm (10 inch) flour tortillas

450 g (1 lb/1¾ cups) chunky tomato salsa

360 g (12¾ oz) grated cheddar cheese

sour cream and guacamole (see page 30), to serve

SERVES 6–8

1  Heat 1 tablespoon of the oil in a large saucepan over medium heat and cook the onion and capsicum for 5 minutes or until softened. Add the garlic and cook for a further 1 minute. Remove from the pan.

2  In the same pan, heat the remaining oil over high heat and cook the beef until brown, breaking up any lumps with a wooden spoon. Add the cumin, paprika and chilli flakes and cook for 1 minute. Stir in the onion mixture, tomato paste and tomatoes. Season with salt and black pepper. Cover, reduce the heat and simmer for 30 minutes. Stir in the beans, then cool.

3  Preheat the oven to 180°C (350°F/Gas 4). Line a large oven tray with baking paper. Spread 1 tablespoon of salsa and 4 tablespoons beef over each tortilla. Roll up to enclose the filling and place on the tray. Spoon the remaining salsa on top and sprinkle with the cheese.

4  Bake for 15 minutes or until the cheese has melted and the enchiladas are heated through. Serve with sour cream, guacamole and a green salad.

# tortilla de patatas (potato tortilla)

**SPAIN** While in Mexico a tortilla is a flat bread made of corn or flour, the Spanish word tortilla means 'flat cake' and refers to an omelette made with eggs and potatoes. This *tortilla de patatas* is one of the most popular dishes served in Spain and can be eaten warm or cold.

4 large all-purpose potatoes, peeled and sliced into 3 mm (⅛ inch) thick slices

8 eggs

80 ml (2½ fl oz/⅓ cup) milk

2 tablespoons olive oil

1 brown onion, finely diced

1 red capsicum (pepper), seeded, membrane removed and finely chopped

1 garlic clove, finely chopped

1 teaspoon sweet paprika, or to taste

⅓ cup chopped flat-leaf (Italian) parsley

**SERVES 6**

1  Cook the potatoes in a large saucepan of boiling salted water for 5 minutes, or until almost tender. Drain.

2  Preheat a grill (broiler) to medium–high. Whisk the eggs and milk together in a large bowl. Season with black pepper. Heat the oil in a frying pan with a heatproof handle over medium–high heat and cook the onion, capsicum, garlic and paprika for 5 minutes, stirring regularly, until the onion has softened. Add the potato, sprinkle with the parsley, then season with salt and black pepper.

3  Pour the egg mixture over the potato and gently shake the pan so the egg mixture spreads evenly in the base. Cook over medium heat, without stirring, for 5 minutes, or until the bottom of the tortilla has set.

4  Place the tortilla in the pan under the preheated grill for 5 minutes, or until set on top. Use a spatula to release the tortilla from the pan and slide it onto a chopping board, then cut it into wedges and serve with a green salad.

# fried rice

**CHINA** Fried rice is known as a peasant food in China, as it is a method of using up leftover cooked rice and vegetables. There are no strict rules when making fried rice except that the rice needs to be cooked and cooled down before stir-frying.

80 ml (2½ fl oz/⅓ cup) peanut oil

3 eggs, lightly beaten

1 brown onion, finely diced

100 g (3½ oz) bacon slices, chopped

2 garlic cloves, crushed

1 tablespoon finely grated fresh ginger

1 teaspoon caster (superfine) sugar

1 tablespoon shaoxing rice wine

740 g (1 lb 10 oz/4 cups) cooked jasmine rice (see note)

80 g (2¾ oz/½ cup) frozen peas, thawed

80 g (2¾ oz/½ cup) frozen corn, thawed

1 tablespoon oyster sauce

4 spring onions (scallions), thinly sliced

½ teaspoon sesame oil

1 tablespoon soy sauce

1 fresh long red chilli, seeded and finely chopped (optional), to serve

SERVES 4–6

1 Heat 1 tablespoon of the oil in a large wok over medium–high heat. Add half the egg and swirl to coat the base and side of the wok, cook for 1 minute or until just set. Remove from the wok, place onto a chopping board and roll up. Repeat with the remaining egg. Thinly slice both egg rolls, set aside.

2 Heat the remaining oil over high heat. Add the onion and bacon and stir-fry for 2 minutes. Add the garlic and ginger and cook for a further 2 minutes.

3 Add the sugar and rice wine, cooking for 1 minute, then add the rice to the wok and cook for 1 minute, stirring to coat.

4 Add the egg, peas, corn, oyster sauce, spring onion, sesame oil and soy sauce and stir-fry for 3 minutes, or until heated through. Serve immediately, sprinkled with chilli, if using.

**Note:** To make the cooked rice you will need to start with 300 g (10½ oz/1½ cups) uncooked rice. Follow the cooking instructions on the packet.

# salad niçoise

**FRANCE** This dish originally got its name from the city of Nice, in Provence, France. The exact ingredients vary between recipes (sometimes it includes boiled potatoes), but it should always feature tuna, anchovy and boiled egg.

3 eggs

175 g (6 oz) green beans, trimmed then halved diagonally

80 ml (2½ fl oz/⅓ cup) olive oil

2 tablespoons white wine vinegar

1 garlic clove, halved

1 baby cos (romaine) lettuce, leaves separated

1 Lebanese (short) cucumber

1 celery stalk

2 ripe tomatoes, cut into wedges

1 small red capsicum (pepper), seeded, membrane removed and thinly sliced

¼ large red onion, thinly sliced

425 g (15 oz) tin tuna in oil, drained and broken into chunks

12 kalamata olives

10 anchovy fillets, drained (optional)

2 teaspoons baby capers, rinsed and drained

12 small basil leaves

**SERVES 4**

1 Put the eggs in a saucepan of cold water. Bring to the boil, then reduce the heat and simmer for 3 minutes. Stir during the first few minutes to centre the yolks. Cool under cold water, then peel and cut into quarters.

2 Cook the beans in a saucepan of boiling water for 2 minutes, or until bright green. Rinse under cold water, then drain.

3 To make the salad dressing, whisk together the oil and vinegar.

4 Rub the garlic over the base and sides of individual plates or a large serving dish and add the lettuce leaves. Cut the cucumber and celery into thin 5 cm (2 inch) lengths. Layer the egg, tomato, beans, cucumber, celery and capsicum over the lettuce. Scatter the onion and tuna over the top, then add the olives, anchovies, capers and basil. Drizzle with the dressing and serve.

# dinnertime

n laksa

**SIA** This spicy curry noodle soup is a tradition of Peranakan culture, merging the
s that are typical of China, with coconut milk, which is a popular ingredient used in
ysian cooking. If you like you can substitute chicken for the prawns.

1 kg (2 lb 4 oz) raw large king prawns (shrimp)

80 ml (2½ fl oz/⅓ cup) vegetable oil

1 teaspoon shrimp paste

2 fresh long red chillies, seeded and finely chopped

1 brown onion, chopped

3 garlic cloves, chopped

2 cm (¾ inch) piece fresh ginger, peeled and quartered

1 teaspoon ground turmeric

1 tablespoon ground coriander

3 lemongrass stems, pale part only, chopped

550 ml (19 fl oz) tin coconut cream

2 teaspoons grated palm sugar (jaggery) or brown sugar

4 kaffir lime (makrut) leaves, centre vein removed, finely shredded

1 teaspoon salt

100 g (3½ oz) fresh thin hokkien (egg) noodles

90 g (3¼ oz) packet fried tofu puffs

90 g (3¼ oz/1 cup) bean sprouts, trimmed

mint and coriander (cilantro) leaves, to serve

lime wedges, to serve

SERVES 4–6

1   Peel and devein the prawns, reserving the shells, heads and tails.

2   Heat 2 tablespoons of the oil in a large heavy-based saucepan and add the prawn shells, heads and tails. Stir until the heads are bright orange, then add 1.25 litres (44 fl oz/5 cups) water. Bring to the boil, reduce the heat, and simmer for 15 minutes. Strain through a sieve, discarding the shells. Clean the pan.

3   Preheat the grill (broiler) to high. Wrap the shrimp paste in a small square of foil to enclose it. Place under the grill for 3 minutes each side or until fragrant. Unwrap the shrimp paste and place in a food processor with the chilli, onion, garlic, ginger, turmeric, coriander, lemongrass and 60 ml (2 fl oz/¼ cup) of the prawn stock. Process until it forms a paste.

4   Heat the remaining oil in the clean saucepan over medium heat and cook the chilli mixture for 3 minutes, stirring until fragrant. Pour in the remaining stock and simmer for 10 minutes, then add the coconut cream, palm sugar, lime leaves and salt. Bring to a simmer and cook gently for 5 minutes.

5   Meanwhile, bring a medium saucepan of water to the boil and cook the noodles for 2 minutes, or until tender. Drain and divide among serving bowls.

6   Add the prawns to the soup and simmer for 1 minute, then add the tofu puffs and cook for 3–5 minutes, or until the prawns just turn pink and the tofu is heated through.

7   Divide the bean sprouts among the bowls and ladle the soup over. Scatter over the mint and coriander, and serve with the lime wedges on the side.

# baby corn and chicken soup

CHINA There are many different kinds of chicken soups and broths made all over the world, but this chicken and corn version is a Chinese favourite and uses many of the popular ingredients of Asian cooking, such as lemongrass, ginger, chilli and soy sauce.

150 g (5½ oz) whole baby corn (see note)

1 tablespoon olive oil

2 lemongrass stems, pale part only, thinly sliced

2 tablespoons grated fresh ginger

6 spring onions (scallions), thinly sliced

1 fresh long red chilli, finely chopped

1 litre (35 fl oz/4 cups) chicken stock

375 ml (13 fl oz/1½ cups) coconut milk

250 g (9 oz) boneless, skinless chicken breasts, thinly sliced

125 g (4½ oz) tin creamed corn

1 tablespoon soy sauce

2 tablespoons snipped chives, to serve

1 fresh long red chilli, thinly sliced lengthways, to serve (optional)

SERVES 4

1 Cut the baby corn in halves or quarters lengthways, depending on their size.

2 Heat the oil in a saucepan over medium heat and cook the lemongrass, ginger, spring onion and chilli, stirring constantly, for 1 minute, or until fragrant.

3 Add the stock and coconut milk to the pan and bring to the boil — do not cover the saucepan or the coconut milk will curdle.

4 Add the corn, chicken and creamed corn and simmer very gently for 5 minutes, or until the chicken is just cooked through.

5 Add the soy sauce, season well with salt and black pepper, and serve the soup in bowls, garnished with the chives and chilli, if using.

**Note:** Tinned baby corn can be substituted for fresh baby corn if fresh is unavailable. Add the tinned corn during the last 2 minutes of cooking.

# minestrone with pesto

**ITALY** There is no strict recipe for this popular Italian soup, which varies by region in its country of origin. You can include a variety of vegetables, meat, pulses and either rice or pasta shells.

60 ml (2 fl oz/¼ cup) olive oil

1 large brown onion, finely chopped

2 garlic cloves, crushed

60 g (2¼ oz) pancetta, finely chopped

1 celery stick, halved and thinly sliced

1 carrot, halved and thinly sliced

1 potato, diced

2 teaspoons tomato paste
(concentrated purée)

400 g (14 oz/1⅔ cups) tin
chopped tomatoes

2 tablespoons torn basil leaves

2 litres (70 fl oz/8 cups) chicken
or vegetable stock

2 zucchini (courgettes), cut into
1.5 cm (⅝ inch) slices

115 g (4 oz/¾ cup) frozen peas

60 g (2¼ oz) green beans,
cut into short lengths

400 g (14 oz/1¾ cups) tin borlotti (cranberry)
beans, rinsed and drained

70 g (2½ oz/¾ cup) ditalini
or other small pasta

80 g (2¾ oz/2 cups) baby spinach leaves

¼ cup chopped flat-leaf (Italian) parsley

**pesto**

2 cups basil leaves

20 g (¾ oz) pine nuts, lightly toasted

2 garlic cloves

100 ml (3½ fl oz) olive oil

25 g (1 oz/¼ cup) finely grated
parmesan cheese

SERVES 6

1 Heat the oil in a large saucepan over low heat. Add the onion, garlic and pancetta and cook for 8–10 minutes, stirring occasionally, until the onion has softened.

2 Add the celery, carrot and potato to the pan and cook for 5 minutes. Stir in the tomato paste, tomatoes and basil. Add the stock and bring slowly to the boil. Simmer for 30 minutes, stirring occasionally, or until reduced slightly.

3 Add the zucchini, peas, green and borlotti beans and pasta and simmer for 8–10 minutes, or until the vegetables are cooked and the pasta is *al dente*. Season with salt and black pepper, to taste.

4 Meanwhile, to make the pesto, put the basil, pine nuts, garlic and a pinch of salt in a food processor and process until finely chopped. With the motor running, slowing add the oil until combined. Transfer to a bowl and stir in the parmesan, seasoning with black pepper, to taste.

5 Just before serving the soup, stir through the spinach and parsley. Spoon into deep serving bowls and add a dollop of pesto on top. Serve with slices of crusty bread on the side.

# salmon and potato cakes

**IRELAND** The Irish consume more potatoes per capita than any other country in the world. Many years ago, under English rule the humble potato provided the starving people of Ireland with a cheap and nutritious meal. Potato cakes with salmon is still a much loved dish today.

700 g (1 lb 9 oz) all-purpose potatoes, peeled and chopped

50 g (1¾ oz) butter

60 ml (2 fl oz/¼ cup) milk

415 g (14¾ oz) tin pink salmon

1 tablespoon baby capers, rinsed and drained

finely grated zest of 1 lemon

1 tablespoon freshly squeezed lemon juice

1 egg, lightly beaten

125 g (4½ oz/1¼ cups) dry breadcrumbs

80 ml (2½ fl oz/⅓ cup) vegetable oil

**SERVES 4**

1 Cook the potatoes in a saucepan of boiling water until very tender. Drain well, transfer to a bowl with the butter and then mash until smooth. Add the milk, season with salt and black pepper, to taste, and use a wooden spoon to beat until well combined.

2 Drain the salmon, place in a medium bowl and use a fork to roughly flake the flesh and bones. Add the potato mixture, capers, lemon zest, lemon juice, egg and 1 tablespoon of the breadcrumbs and mix well to combine.

3 Spread the remaining breadcrumbs onto a large plate. Take ¼ cup of the potato mixture at a time and use your hands to shape a 6 cm (2½ inch) round patty, about 2 cm (¾ inch) thick. Dust the patty with breadcrumbs to coat. Repeat to make 12 patties in total. Refrigerate for 30 minutes.

4 Heat the oil in a large frying pan over medium–high heat. Cook the patties, in batches, for 4 minutes on each side, or until golden brown and heated through. Serve with a salad and tartare sauce on the side.

# pastitsio (meat and pasta bake)

**GREECE** This typically Greek dish is influenced by the Italians, and resembles a lasagne, although instead of using sheets of pasta, this recipe calls for macaroni pasta.

150 g (5½ oz/1 cup) elbow macaroni

40 g (1½ oz) butter

¼ teaspoon ground nutmeg

60 g (2¼ oz/⅔ cup) grated kefalotyri or parmesan cheese

1 egg, lightly beaten

**meat sauce**

2 tablespoons olive oil

1 brown onion, finely chopped

2 garlic cloves, crushed

500 g (1 lb 2 oz) minced (ground) beef

375 ml (13 fl oz/1½ cups) beef stock

60 g (2¼ oz/¼ cup) tomato paste (concentrated purée)

½ teaspoon dried oregano

**bechamel sauce**

40 g (1½ oz) butter

1½ tablespoons plain (all-purpose) flour

375 ml (13 fl oz/1½ cups) milk

pinch of ground nutmeg

1 egg, lightly beaten

SERVES 6

1   Preheat the oven to 180°C (350°F/Gas 4). Lightly grease a 1.5 litre (52 fl oz/6 cup) ovenproof dish.

2   Cook the macaroni in a large saucepan of boiling salted water for 10 minutes, or until *al dente*. Drain and return to the pan. Melt the butter in a small saucepan, then pour it over the macaroni. Stir in the nutmeg and half of the cheese and season with salt and black pepper, to taste. Cool, then mix in the egg and set aside.

3   To make the meat sauce, heat the oil in a large frying pan over medium heat. Add the onion and garlic and cook for 8 minutes, or until the onion has softened. Increase the heat, add the beef and cook for 5 minutes, or until the meat has browned. Add the stock, tomato paste and oregano, cover, and simmer for 20 minutes.

4   Meanwhile, make the béchamel sauce. Melt the butter in a small saucepan over low heat. Stir in the flour and cook for 1 minute, or until foaming. Remove from the heat and gradually stir in the milk. Return to the heat and stir constantly until the sauce boils and thickens. Reduce the heat and simmer for 2 minutes, then add the nutmeg and season, to taste. Allow to cool a little before stirring in the egg. Stir 3 tablespoons of the béchamel into the meat sauce.

5   Spread half of the meat sauce in the dish, then layer over half of the pasta. Add another layer each of meat and pasta, pressing down firmly with the back of a spoon to flatten. Spread the béchamel sauce over the pasta and sprinkle the remaining cheese on top.

6   Bake for 45–50 minutes, or until golden. Let it stand for 15 minutes before slicing and serving.

**Note:** Tubular pasta, which is available in varying thicknesses, can be used as a substitute for the elbow macaroni.

# osso bucco with gremolata

**ITALY** The name of this dish literally translates from the Italian as 'bone with a hole' or marrowbone, which refers to the cut of veal that is also used in this popular dish from Milan. The veal is sautéed on the bone and braised with tomato, garlic and onion.

2 tablespoons olive oil

1 brown onion, finely chopped

1 garlic clove, crushed

1 kg (2 lb 4 oz) veal shin slices (osso bucco)

2 tablespoons plain (all-purpose) flour

400 g (14 oz/1⅔ cups) tin chopped tomatoes

500 ml (17 fl oz/2 cups) chicken stock

### gremolata

2 tablespoons finely chopped flat-leaf (Italian) parsley

1 lemon, zest finely shredded or grated

1 garlic clove, finely chopped

SERVES 4

1 Heat half of the oil in a large heavy-based saucepan over low heat. Add the onion and cook for 10 minutes, or until softened. Add the garlic and cook for 1 minute or until fragrant. Remove to a plate and set aside.

2 Heat the remaining oil in the same saucepan. Add the veal, in batches, and brown over medium–high heat for 6–7 minutes, turning once. Transfer the veal to a plate and set aside.

3 Return the onion to the pan and stir in the flour. Cook for 30 seconds, then remove from the heat and slowly stir in the tomatoes and stock until well combined. Return the veal to the pan and bring to the boil, stirring occasionally. Reduce the heat to low, cover, and simmer for 2 hours, or until the meat is very tender and almost falling off the bone.

4 To make the gremolata, mix together all of the ingredients in a bowl.

5 Serve the osso bucco sprinkled with the gremolata, and accompanied with steamed rice.

# pad thai

**THAILAND** This popular dish made with rice noodles was thought to have been brought to the ancient Thai capital, Ayutthaya, by Vietnamese traders. It became popular in the 1930s and 1940s when the prime minister wanted to reduce the rice imports into the country.

250 g (9 oz) dried rice stick noodles

1 tablespoon tamarind purée

1 small fresh red chilli, chopped

2 garlic cloves, finely chopped

2 spring onions (scallions), sliced

1½ tablespoons finely grated palm sugar (jaggery) or brown sugar

2 tablespoons fish sauce

2 tablespoons freshly squeezed lime juice

2 tablespoons peanut oil

2 eggs, beaten

150 g (5½ oz) pork fillet, thinly sliced

8 raw large prawns (shrimp), peeled and deveined

100 g (3½ oz) fried tofu puffs, thinly sliced

90 g (3¼ oz/1 cup) bean sprouts, trimmed

40 g (1½ oz/¼ cup) chopped roasted peanuts

¼ cup coriander (cilantro) leaves

lime wedges, to serve

**SERVES 4**

1  Put the noodles in a heatproof bowl, cover with warm water and soak for 15–20 minutes, or until soft and pliable. Drain well.

2  Combine the tamarind purée with 1 tablespoon water. Put the chilli, garlic and spring onion in a small food processor, spice grinder or use a mortar and pestle and grind to a smooth paste. Transfer the mixture to a bowl. Stir in the tamarind mixture, then add the palm sugar, fish sauce and lime juice, stirring well to combine.

3  Heat 1 tablespoon of the oil in a wok over high heat and swirl to coat the base and side. Add the egg, swirl to coat and cook for 1–2 minutes, or until set into an omelette. Remove from the wok, roll up and cut into thin slices.

4  Heat the remaining oil in the wok, stir in the chilli mixture and stir-fry for 30 seconds or until fragrant. Add the pork and prawns and stir-fry for 2 minutes, or until the pork is just tender and the prawns have turned pink and are just cooked through.

5  Add the noodles, egg, tofu and bean sprouts to the wok and gently toss everything together until heated through. Serve immediately, sprinkled with the peanuts and the coriander and lime wedges on the side.

# garithes yiouvetsi (baked prawns with feta)

**GREECE** This tasty dish is easy to make and uses some of the best-known ingredients from its country of origin — fresh prawns from the sea, in-season tomatoes and feta cheese, a popular Greek cheese that has a sharp, salty flavour. The Greeks love to cook their prawns this way.

2 tablespoons olive oil

1 large red onion, finely chopped

1 garlic clove, crushed

700 g (1 lb 9 oz) ripe tomatoes, diced

80 ml (2½ fl oz/⅓ cup) freshly squeezed lemon juice

⅓ cup oregano leaves or 1 teaspoon dried oregano

20 raw large king prawns (shrimp), peeled and deveined, tails left intact

120 g (4¼ oz) feta cheese

2 tablespoons extra virgin olive oil, for drizzling

chopped flat-leaf (Italian) parsley, to serve

**SERVES 4**

1 Preheat the oven to 180°C (350°F/Gas 4).

2 Heat the olive oil in a saucepan over medium heat. Cook the onion, stirring occasionally, for 5 minutes, or until softened. Add the garlic and cook for 1 minute. Add the tomato and cook for 10 minutes, or until the mixture is slightly reduced and thickened. Stir in the lemon juice and oregano, then season to taste with salt and black pepper.

3 Pour the sauce into four 375 ml (13 fl oz/ 1½ cup) ovenproof dishes. Place five prawns in each dish over the sauce and crumble over the feta cheese. Drizzle with the extra virgin olive oil and sprinkle with a little more black pepper, to taste.

4 Bake for 30 minutes, or until the prawns turn pink and are just cooked. Serve immediately with salad and crusty bread on the side.

# penne alla napolitana

**ITALY** *Napolitana* sauce is a vegetarian sauce recipe originating in Naples, Italy. It is a mainstay of the southern regions of the country, attributed to the times when meat was scarce. These days the name applies to any simple tomato sauce flavoured with onion, basil and parsley.

2 tablespoons olive oil

1 brown onion, finely chopped

1 small carrot, finely diced

1 celery stick, finely diced

2 garlic cloves, finely chopped

800 g (1 lb 12 oz/3¼ cups) tin chopped tomatoes

1 tablespoon tomato paste (concentrated purée)

¼ cup shredded basil leaves

500 g (1 lb 2 oz) penne pasta

coarsely grated parmesan cheese

SERVES 4–6

1 Heat the oil in a large frying pan over medium heat. Cook the onion for 5 minutes, or until it starts to soften. Add the carrot and celery and cook for a further 5 minutes, then add the garlic and cook for 1 minute.

2 Add the tomatoes and tomato paste to the pan. Bring to a simmer and cook gently for about 20 minutes, stirring occasionally, until the sauce thickens. Stir in the basil and season with salt and black pepper, to taste.

3 Meanwhile, cook the pasta in a saucepan of boiling salted water for 8–10 minutes, or until *al dente*. Drain well and return to the pan. Add the sauce to the pasta and mix well.

4 Serve in bowls, sprinkled with the parmesan and accompanied by a garden salad.

# nasi goreng

**INDONESIA** Literally translating as 'fried rice' in Indonesia, *nasi goreng* is the national dish. As in this recipe, *Nasi goreng* is typically seasoned with kecap manis, a thick, intensely flavoured, sweet Indonesian soy sauce.

2 teaspoons shrimp paste

2 fresh long red chillies, seeded and finely chopped

8 garlic cloves, finely chopped

vegetable oil, for cooking

2 eggs, lightly beaten

350 g (12 oz) boneless, skinless chicken thighs, cut into thin strips

200 g (7 oz) raw prawns (shrimp), peeled and deveined, tails left intact

1.5 kg (3 lb 5 oz/8 cups) cold cooked rice (see note)

80 ml (2½ fl oz/⅓ cup) kecap manis

2 tablespoons soy sauce

2 Lebanese (short) cucumbers, chopped

1 large ripe tomato, chopped

lime wedges, to serve

**SERVES 6**

1 Preheat the grill (broiler) to high. Wrap the shrimp paste in a small square of foil to enclose it. Place under the grill and heat for 3 minutes on each side, or until fragrant. Process the shrimp paste, chilli and garlic in a small food processor until a paste forms.

2 Heat 1 tablespoon of the oil in a wok over high heat and swirl to coat the base and side. Add the egg, swirl to coat and cook for 1–2 minutes, or until set into an omelette. Remove from the wok, roll up and cut into thin slices.

3 Heat 1 tablespoon of the oil in the wok over high heat and stir-fry the chicken and half of the chilli paste for 3–4 minutes, or until the chicken is just cooked. Remove the chicken from the wok.

4 Heat 1 tablespoon of the oil in the wok and stir-fry the prawns and the remaining chilli paste for 2–3 minutes, or until the prawns change colour and are just cooked. Remove from the wok and set aside.

5 Heat 1 tablespoon of the oil in the wok over medium heat. Add the rice and toss for 4–5 minutes, or until heated through. Add the kecap manis and soy sauce and toss constantly until all of the rice is coated in the sauces. Return the chicken and prawns to the wok, and toss to heat through. Transfer to a serving bowl and top with the omelette strips, cucumber and tomato. Serve with the lime wedges.

**Note:** It is a good idea to cook the rice the day before so that it dries out a little. Spread it in a shallow dish, cover, and refrigerate.

# lamb kefta (lamb meatballs)

**MOROCCO** This version of lamb meatballs has its origins in North Africa and is known as kefta ghan' mi bel'. The lamb mince is mixed together with a tasty assortment of fresh herbs and spices then baked and served with a spicy tomato and harissa-spiced sauce.

1 kg (2 lb 4 oz) minced (ground) lamb

1 brown onion, finely chopped

2 garlic cloves, finely chopped

2 tablespoons finely chopped flat-leaf (Italian) parsley leaves

2 tablespoons finely chopped coriander (cilantro) leaves

½ teaspoon cayenne pepper

½ teaspoon ground allspice

½ teaspoon ground ginger

½ teaspoon ground cardamom

1 teaspoon ground cumin

1 teaspoon paprika

**sauce**

2 tablespoons olive oil

1 brown onion, finely chopped

2 garlic cloves, finely chopped

2 teaspoons ground cumin

½ teaspoon ground cinnamon

1 teaspoon paprika

800 g (1 lb 12 oz/3¼ cups) tin chopped tomatoes

2 teaspoons harissa

⅓ cup chopped coriander (cilantro) leaves

SERVES 4–6

1  Preheat the oven to 180°C (350°F/Gas 4). Lightly grease two baking trays.

2  Place the lamb, onion, garlic, parsley, coriander, cayenne pepper, allspice, ginger, cardamom, cumin and paprika in a bowl and mix well. Season with salt and black pepper. Take a heaped teaspoon of the mixture at a time and roll into balls. Place on the prepared trays and bake for 15 minutes, or until browned.

3  Meanwhile, to make the sauce, heat the oil in a large frying pan over medium heat. Cook the onion for 8 minutes, or until softened. Add the garlic, cumin, cinnamon and paprika, and cook for 1 minute, or until fragrant. Stir in the tomatoes and harissa and bring to the boil. Reduce the heat to low and simmer for 20 minutes. Taste and season with salt and black pepper, as needed.

4  Add the meatballs to the pan and simmer in the sauce for 10 minutes, or until warmed through. Stir in the coriander, season well and serve the meatballs and sauce with couscous.

# satay chicken

INDONESIA Satay is the name given to dishes of marinated, skewered and grilled meats served with a sauce. In Indonesia and other Southeast Asian countries, where this dish was made originally, the satay skewers are served with a delicious peanut sauce.

500 g (1 lb 2 oz) boneless, skinless chicken thighs

1 brown onion, chopped

2 lemongrass stems, pale part only, thinly sliced

4 garlic cloves

2 fresh long red chillies, seeded and chopped

2 teaspoons ground coriander

1 teaspoon ground cumin

½ teaspoon salt

1 tablespoon soft brown sugar

1 tablespoon soy sauce

peanut oil, for cooking

**peanut sauce**

165 g (5¾ oz/⅔ cup) crunchy peanut butter

250 ml (9 fl oz/1 cup) coconut milk

1–2 tablespoons sweet chilli sauce

1 tablespoon soy sauce

2 teaspoons freshly squeezed lemon juice

SERVES 4

1 Soak 16 wooden skewers in cold water for 30 minutes to prevent them from burning during cooking.

2 Cut the chicken into thick flat strips and thread onto the skewers.

3 Put the onion, lemongrass, garlic, chilli, coriander, cumin, salt, sugar, soy sauce and 1 tablespoon of the peanut oil in a food processor and process until smooth. Spread the mixture over the chicken, cover with plastic wrap and refrigerate for 30 minutes.

4 To make the peanut sauce, combine all of the ingredients in a saucepan with 125 ml (4 fl oz/½ cup) water. Stir over medium heat until the mixture boils. Remove from the heat — the sauce will thicken while standing.

5 Brush a chargrill pan or barbecue flat plate with oil and heat until very hot. Cook the skewers, in batches if necessary, for 2–3 minutes on each side.

6 Serve the chicken skewers with the peanut sauce, cucumber sticks with chopped peanuts, and jasmine rice, if desired.

# potato gnocchi with tomato sauce

**ITALY** The first recipe for gnocchi originated in the 1300s when these small dumplings were made with semolina flour. It was only much later, in the 1500s, that potato was used in the recipe. The word *gnoccho* means 'lump' in Italian, which reflects the way the gnocchi looks.

500 g (1 lb 2 oz) packet potato gnocchi

freshly grated parmesan cheese, to serve

**tomato sauce**

1 kg (2 lb 4 oz) tomatoes, peeled and chopped

2 garlic cloves, crushed

125 ml (4 fl oz/½ cup) vegetable or chicken stock

¼ cup finely chopped basil leaves

1 teaspoon sugar, or to taste

**SERVES 4**

1   To make the sauce, place the tomato, garlic and stock in a saucepan over high heat and bring to the boil. Reduce the heat and simmer for 20–25 minutes, stirring occasionally, until the sauce thickens slightly. Stir through the basil and season with the sugar, salt and black pepper, to taste.

2   Cook the gnocchi in a large saucepan of boiling water until cooked — they will float to the surface when ready. Drain well.

3   Add the warm gnocchi to the sauce and use a large metal spoon or spatula to stir gently to coat. Serve in warmed bowls, sprinkled with the parmesan and accompanied by salad and bread.

# carrot and pumpkin risotto

**ITALY** The name risotto means 'little rice' and is one of the most popular ways of cooking this staple in Italy — it is cooked slowly in stock and needs to be stirred constantly in the saucepan so the rice cooks evenly and ends up with a lovely creamy consistency.

90 g (3¼ oz) unsalted butter

1 brown onion, finely chopped

400 g (14 oz) pumpkin (winter squash), peeled, seeded and cut into 1 cm (½ inch) pieces

3 carrots, cut into 1 cm (½ inch) pieces

2 litres (70 fl oz/8 cups) vegetable or chicken stock

440 g (15½ oz/2 cups) arborio rice

100 g (3½ oz/1 cup) grated parmesan cheese

¼ teaspoon ground nutmeg

½ teaspoon thyme leaves

SERVES 6

1   Heat 60 g (2¼ oz) of the butter in a heavy-based saucepan over medium heat. Cook the onion for 3 minutes, or until softened, then add the pumpkin and carrot and cook for 6–8 minutes, or until the vegetables start to soften. Roughly mash the vegetables.

2   Meanwhile, bring the stock to the boil in a separate saucepan. Keep at a gentle simmer.

3   Add the rice to the vegetables and cook for 1–2 minutes, stirring. Add 125 ml (4 fl oz/ ½ cup) of the stock and cook, stirring constantly, until all the liquid is absorbed. Continue adding the stock, ½ cup at a time, stirring constantly and making sure the stock is absorbed before adding more. Cook for 20–25 minutes, or until the rice is tender but firm to the bite and the mixture is creamy.

4   Remove from the heat, then stir in the remaining butter, the parmesan, nutmeg and thyme. Serve immediately.

# singapore noodles

**CHINA** Nobody can really agree on where this noodle dish originated, although it is highly likely that a version of it started in China many generations ago. These days it is a regular feature on menus all over the world.

150 g (5½ oz) dried rice vermicelli

250 g (9 oz) Chinese barbecued pork (char siu)

vegetable oil, for cooking

250 g (9 oz) raw king prawns (shrimp), peeled, deveined and cut into small pieces

1½ tablespoons madras curry powder

2 garlic cloves, crushed

1 brown onion, cut into thin wedges

100 g (3½ oz) shiitake mushrooms, sliced

100 g (3½ oz) green beans, thinly sliced

1 tablespoon soy sauce

4 spring onions (scallions), thinly sliced

SERVES 4–6

1  Place the vermicelli in a large bowl, cover with boiling water and soak for 5 minutes. Drain well and spread on paper towel or a clean tea towel (dish towel) to drain.

2  Thinly slice the pork into even-sized pieces. Heat 1 tablespoon of the oil in a wok over medium–high heat and swirl to coat the base and side. Stir-fry the pork and the prawn pieces, in batches, for 2 minutes, or until the prawn just turns pink and is cooked through. Remove from the wok and set aside.

3  Heat 2 tablespoons of the oil in the wok over medium heat. Stir-fry the curry powder and garlic for 1–2 minutes, or until fragrant. Add the onion and mushroom, and stir-fry for 2–3 minutes, or until the onion and mushroom are soft.

4  Return the pork and prawns to the wok, add the beans and 125 ml (4 fl oz/½ cup) water, and toss to combine. Cook for 3 minutes, or until the beans turn bright green. Add the drained noodles, soy sauce and spring onion, toss well to combine and serve immediately.

# southern indian fish curry

**INDIA** Indian curries are world-renowned for their wonderfully spicy flavours and bright colours. This fish curry is typical of the southern regions of India, using coconut milk, tomatoes and a mix of spices, including cinnamon, turmeric and chilli.

1 tablespoon vegetable oil

1 brown onion, cut into thin wedges

2 garlic cloves, crushed

5 cm (2 inch) piece fresh ginger, grated

2 teaspoons ground coriander

1 teaspoon ground turmeric

¼ teaspoon chilli powder

1 cinnamon stick

400 g (14 oz/1⅔ cups) tin chopped tomatoes

250 ml (9 fl oz/1 cup) vegetable or fish stock

80 ml (2½ fl oz/⅓ cup) coconut milk

600 g (1 lb 5 oz) boneless, skinless firm white fish fillets, cut into 2.5 cm (1 inch) pieces

100 g (3½ oz/2 cups) baby spinach leaves

**SERVES 4**

1 Heat the oil in a large saucepan over medium heat. Cook the onion for 8 minutes, or until softened. Add the garlic, ginger, coriander, turmeric, chilli and cinnamon and cook, stirring, for 2–3 minutes, or until fragrant. Add the tomatoes, stock and coconut milk and bring to the boil, then reduce the heat and simmer for 15 minutes.

2 Add the fish pieces and simmer gently for 2 minutes, then gently stir through the spinach leaves and cook for 1–2 minutes longer, or until the fish is just cooked through and the spinach is wilted and bright green. Season with salt and black pepper. Serve with steamed basmati rice and lemon wedges on the side.

# beef and hokkien noodles

**CHINA** Although hokkien noodles originated in China, they also feature on many menus in Malaysia and Singapore — it is believed that Chinese immigrants brought the hokkien noodles from the Fujian province in southeast China. They are terrific used in stir-fries.

350 g (12 oz) rump steak

100 g (3½ oz) snow peas (mangetout)

600 g (1 lb 5 oz) fresh hokkien (egg) noodles

2 tablespoons peanut oil

1 large brown onion, cut into thin wedges

1 large carrot, halved and thinly sliced

1 red capsicum (pepper), seeded, membrane removed and cut into thin strips

2 garlic cloves, crushed

1 teaspoon grated fresh ginger

200 g (7 oz) shiitake mushrooms, sliced

60 ml (2 fl oz/¼ cup) oyster sauce

2 tablespoons light soy sauce

1 tablespoon soft brown sugar

½ teaspoon Chinese five-spice

**SERVES 4**

1 Cut the steak across the grain into thin slices. Top and tail the snow peas and slice in half diagonally. Soak the noodles in a large bowl of boiling water for 10 minutes.

2 Heat half of the oil in a wok over high heat. Stir-fry the steak quickly, in batches, until just browned. Remove to a plate and set aside.

3 Heat the remaining oil in the wok over high heat. Stir-fry the onion, carrot and capsicum for 2–3 minutes, or until tender. Add the garlic, ginger, snow peas and shiitake mushrooms and cook for a further 1 minute.

4 Separate the noodles with a fork, then drain. Add to the wok with the steak, tossing well. Combine the oyster sauce with the soy sauce, sugar, five-spice and 1 tablespoon water and pour over the noodles. Toss together until the noodles have warmed through and are coated in the sauce. Serve immediately.

# miso yakitori chicken

**JAPAN** *Yakitori* is the Japanese word for 'grilled fowl', and usually refers to small pieces of chicken that have been skewered and grilled. Miso is another popular ingredient in Japanese food — it is sold in paste form and is made from fermented tofu and grains.

80 ml (2½ fl oz/⅓ cup) mirin

70 g (2½ oz/¼ cup) red miso paste

2 tablespoons sugar

1 kg (2 lb 4 oz) boneless, skinless chicken thighs, trimmed

12 spring onions (scallions)

SERVES 4

1   Soak 16 wooden skewers in cold water for 30 minutes to prevent them from burning during cooking.

2   Place the mirin, miso and sugar in a small saucepan. Stir over medium heat for 2 minutes, or until smooth. Remove from the heat.

3   Cut the chicken into 2.5 cm (1 inch) pieces. Cut the pale section of the spring onions into 4 cm (1½ inch) lengths. Thread the chicken and spring onion alternately onto the skewers.

4   Brush a chargrill pan or barbecue flat plate with oil and heat until very hot. Cook the skewers, turning occasionally, for 8 minutes, or until the chicken is almost cooked. Brush with the miso sauce and continue cooking for another 3 minutes. Turn the skewers over, brush with the miso sauce and cook for a further 3 minutes or until the chicken is cooked through. Serve with steamed rice and stir-fried or steamed Asian greens.

# spaghetti bolognese

**ITALY** This famous pasta sauce originated in Bologna in Italy, where it is traditionally served with tagliatelle pasta. The original 'ragu', or sauce, is made mostly from meat with a little fresh tomato for flavouring, although many Western versions of the sauce use tinned tomatoes as well.

1 tablespoon olive oil

1 large brown onion, finely chopped

3 garlic cloves, crushed

1 celery stick, diced

1 carrot, diced

500 g (1 lb 2 oz) minced (ground) beef

500 ml (17 fl oz/2 cups) beef stock

2 tablespoons tomato paste
(concentrated purée)

800 g (1 lb 12 oz) tin chopped tomatoes

1 tablespoon dried oregano

350 g (12 oz) spaghetti

grated parmesan cheese, to serve

**SERVES 4**

1   Heat the oil in a saucepan over medium heat. Cook the onion for 2–3 minutes, or until softened. Add the garlic, celery and carrot and cook for 2–3 minutes, or until softened.

2   Add the beef and cook over high heat for 5 minutes, or until browned, breaking up any lumps with a wooden spoon. Add the stock, tomato paste, undrained tomatoes and oregano and stir well; season with salt and black pepper.

3   Reduce the heat and simmer for 1 hour, stirring occasionally to prevent it from catching on the base of the pan, or until reduced to a good sauce consistency.

4   Cook the pasta in a large saucepan of boiling water following the packet directions, or until *al dente*. Drain well and then return the pasta to the saucepan. Add the bolognese sauce and toss gently to combine. Serve with the parmesan sprinkled on top.

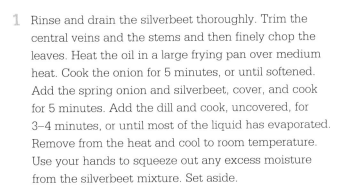

# spanakopita (silverbeet and cheese filo pie)

**GREECE** This traditional silverbeet and cheese pie is made using filo pastry and is often eaten as a snack in Greece, although cut into larger slices it makes a wonderful dinner or lunch. If you can find it, use kefalotyri cheese, which is the Greek version of parmesan cheese.

1.5 kg (3 lb 5 oz) silverbeet (Swiss chard)

3 tablespoons olive oil

1 white onion, finely chopped

10 spring onions (scallions), chopped

1½ tablespoons chopped dill

200 g (7 oz/1⅓ cups) crumbled Greek feta cheese

125 g (4½ oz/½ cup) cottage cheese

3 tablespoons finely grated kefalotyri or parmesan cheese

¼ teaspoon ground nutmeg

4 eggs, lightly beaten

10 sheets filo pastry

80 g (2¾ oz) butter, melted, for brushing

**SERVES 4–6**

1   Rinse and drain the silverbeet thoroughly. Trim the central veins and the stems and then finely chop the leaves. Heat the oil in a large frying pan over medium heat. Cook the onion for 5 minutes, or until softened. Add the spring onion and silverbeet, cover, and cook for 5 minutes. Add the dill and cook, uncovered, for 3–4 minutes, or until most of the liquid has evaporated. Remove from the heat and cool to room temperature. Use your hands to squeeze out any excess moisture from the silverbeet mixture. Set aside.

2   Preheat the oven to 180°C (350°F/Gas 4). Lightly grease a 20 cm (8 inch) square ovenproof dish. Place the feta, cottage and kefalotyri cheeses in a large bowl. Stir in the silverbeet mixture and the nutmeg. Gradually add the eggs and combine well; season with salt and black pepper, to taste.

3   Take one sheet of filo and line the base and sides of the baking dish. Cover the filo with a slightly damp tea towel (dish towel) to prevent them from drying out. Brush with butter and cover with another sheet of filo. Butter the sheet and repeat in this way, using five sheets of pastry. Spoon the filling into the dish and level the surface. Fold the exposed pastry up and over to cover the top of the filling. Cover with a sheet of pastry, brush with butter and continue layering until all the sheets are used. Trim the pastry with kitchen scissors then tuck the excess inside the side of the dish.

4   Brush the top with butter. Using a sharp knife, score the surface into squares. Sprinkle a few drops of cold water on top (this will discourage the pastry from drying out and curling during baking). Bake in the oven for 35–40 minutes, or until golden. Stand at room temperature for 10 minutes before slicing into squares and serving.

# lamb pilaf

**TURKEY** Pilaf is the general name given to seasoned rice dishes served throughout the Middle East. Served with eggplant, lamb meatballs, tomatoes and pistachios this fragrant pilaf makes a wonderful dinner, evoking the best flavours of Turkish cuisine.

100 ml (3½ fl oz) olive oil

1 large eggplant (aubergine), cut into 1 cm (½ inch) cubes

1 large brown onion, finely chopped

1 teaspoon ground cinnamon

2 teaspoons ground cumin

1 teaspoon ground coriander

300 g (10½ oz/1½ cups) basmati rice

500 ml (17 fl oz/2 cups) chicken or vegetable stock

500 g (1 lb 2 oz) minced (ground) lamb

½ teaspoon ground allspice

2 ripe tomatoes, seeded and finely diced

35 g (1¼ oz/¼ cup) toasted pistachios, coarsely chopped

2 tablespoons currants

2 tablespoons chopped coriander (cilantro) leaves

**SERVES 4**

1 Heat 2 tablespoons of the oil in a large, deep, frying pan over medium–high heat. Cook the eggplant for 10 minutes, or until golden and tender. Remove and drain on paper towels.

2 Heat 2 tablespoons of the oil in the same pan over medium heat. Cook the onion for 8 minutes, or until softened. Stir in half of the cinnamon, half the cumin and half the ground coriander, then add the rice and stir to coat with the spices and oil. Pour in the stock, season with salt and black pepper and bring to the boil. Reduce the heat to low, cover, and cook for 15 minutes, or until the rice is tender and small steam holes appear on the surface of the rice. Remove from the heat and stand for 5 minutes before stirring with a fork to separate the grains. Transfer to a bowl and keep warm.

3 Meanwhile, put the lamb in a bowl with the allspice and remaining cumin, cinnamon and ground coriander. Season with salt and black pepper and mix well. Roll the mixture into small balls.

4 Heat the remaining oil in the same frying pan over medium heat and cook the meatballs in batches for 10 minutes, turning often to brown all over. Drain on paper towels.

5 Add the tomato to the same pan and cook for 2 minutes, or until softened. Stir in the eggplant, pistachios, currants, meatballs and rice, stirring well to combine and heat through. Serve the pilaf sprinkled with the coriander.

# thai red vegetable curry

**THAILAND** The three most widely used curry pastes in Thailand are red, green and yellow. Red curry paste is made using red chillies, which give it its colour as well as an unforgettable spicy flavour.

1 tablespoon peanut oil

250 g (9 oz) broccoli florets, quartered

250 g (9 oz) cauliflower florets, quartered

500 g (1 lb 2 oz) orange sweet potato, peeled and cut into 1 cm (½ inch) pieces

2 tablespoons Thai red curry paste

500 ml (17 fl oz/2 cups) coconut milk

1 tablespoon freshly squeezed lime juice, or to taste

1 tablespoon fish sauce, or to taste

3 tablespoons chopped coriander (cilantro) leaves

SERVES 4

1 Heat the oil in a wok over high heat and swirl to coat the base and side. Add the broccoli, cauliflower and sweet potato, in batches, and stir-fry for 3 minutes, or until the vegetables are starting to soften. Return all of the vegetables to the wok. Add 60 ml (2 fl oz/¼ cup) water, reduce the heat to low, cover, and cook for 5 minutes, or until the vegetables are tender.

2 Add the curry paste and cook over medium heat for 1 minute, or until fragrant. Stir in the coconut milk and simmer for 5 minutes, or until the sauce is slightly thickened and the vegetables are tender.

3 Stir through the lime juice, fish sauce and coriander. Serve the curry with steamed jasmine rice.

# beef pies

AUSTRALIA Nearly every country in the world has its own version of a pie — in South America they have empanadas, in Turkey it's *börek*, and the Polish love their *pierozki*. In Australia the most popular type of pie is beef and over 500,000,000 are sold each year!

6 sheets frozen shortcrust pastry, thawed

1 egg yolk, whisked with 2 teaspoons water

**filling**

1.5 kg (3 lb 5 oz) chuck steak

2 tablespoons olive oil

1 large brown onion, finely chopped

1 large carrot, finely chopped

2 garlic cloves, crushed

2 tablespoons plain (all-purpose) flour

500 ml (17 fl oz/2 cups) beef stock

1 tablespoon Worcestershire sauce

2 teaspoons thyme leaves

SERVES 6

1  To make the filling, trim the steak and cut into 1 cm (½ inch) pieces. Heat half of the oil in a frying pan over high heat. Cook the beef, in batches, for 4–5 minutes, or until browned. Remove from the pan and set aside. Add the remaining oil to the pan and cook the onion and carrot over medium heat for 8 minutes or until softened. Add the garlic and cook for 1 minute.

2  Return the meat to the pan and stir in the flour. Stir for 1 minute. Stir in the stock, 250 ml (9 fl oz/1 cup) water, the Worcestershire sauce and the thyme.

3  Bring to a simmer, reduce the heat to very low, cover and simmer gently for 1¼ hours, stirring frequently, or until the meat is very tender. Add a little more water during cooking if needed to keep the meat just covered with liquid. Remove the lid and simmer until the sauce is thick. Remove from the heat and cool completely. Season with salt and black pepper.

4  Preheat the oven to 200°C (400°F/Gas 6). Lightly grease six 9.5 cm (3¾ inch) round pie tins. Lay the pastry on a chopping board and, using the pie tins as a guide, cut out six rounds large enough to line the tins and six round large enough for the lids of the pies. Line the pie tins with the pastry, trimming any excess pastry with a sharp knife. Brush the edges of the pastry with a little water. Spoon the cooled meat filling into the pastry cases. Place a pastry lid over each pie to cover the filling and gently pinch around the edge to seal. Cut a cross in the centre of each pie to allow the steam to escape and place on an oven tray.

5  Lightly brush the pie tops with the egg yolk mixture. Bake for 40 minutes, or until the pastry is golden and cooked through. Cool slightly before removing the pies from the tins. Serve with salad or vegetables.

# chargrilled prawn and chorizo skewers

SPAIN  These simple skewers bring together the well-known flavours of Spanish cuisine — pork (chorizo sausage), seafood (prawns) and peppers (capsicum and paprika). Spanish paprika (sweet, spicy or smoked) is the spice which gives chorizo its distinctive flavour.

olive oil, for greasing

2 Spanish chorizo sausages

2 tablespoons olive oil

1 teaspoon smoked paprika

12 raw large king prawns (shrimp), peeled and deveined, tails left intact

2 green capsicums (peppers), seeded, membrane removed and cut into 3 cm (1¼ inch) pieces

lime wedges, to serve

SERVES 4

1  Soak 12 bamboo skewers in water for 30 minutes to prevent them from burning during cooking.

2  Brush a chargrill pan or barbecue grill with oil. Cut each chorizo sausage into 1 cm (½ inch) thick slices (you should have 24 slices). Cook each slice over high heat for 1 minute each side. Remove to a plate.

3  In a small bowl, combine the olive oil and smoked paprika. Thread the chorizo slices, prawns and capsicum pieces alternately onto the skewers. Season with black pepper and brush with the smoked paprika oil.

4  Cook the skewers over high heat for 3 minutes each side, or until the prawns turn pink and are just cooked through. Serve with lime wedges, a green salad and crusty bread.

# wiener schnitzel

AUSTRIA This is a traditional Austrian dish; *wiener* means Viennese (from Vienna in Austria). According to legend, this dish comes from the 7th century Byzantine Empire where Kaiser Basileios had his meat covered in gold dust. As you can imagine, this eventually became too expensive so they used 'yellow gold' breadcrumbs instead.

125 g (4½ oz/1¼ cups) dry breadcrumbs

¼ cup flat-leaf (Italian) parsley leaves, finely chopped

2 eggs

75 g (2¾ oz/½ cup) plain (all-purpose) flour

4 x 100 g (3½ oz) veal scaloppine (escalopes)

125 ml (4 fl oz/½ cup) olive oil

lemon wedges, to serve

**potato salad**

600 g (1 lb 5 oz) new potatoes, halved

90 g (3¼ oz/⅓ cup) light sour cream

2 tablespoons freshly squeezed lemon juice

¼ cup flat-leaf (Italian) parsley leaves, finely chopped

pinch of sugar

SERVES 4

1 Combine the breadcrumbs and parsley in a shallow bowl. Place the eggs in a separate shallow bowl and whisk lightly to combine. Place the flour in a third shallow bowl and season with salt and black pepper.

2 Place the veal on a chopping board and flatten evenly with a meat mallet or rolling pin until about 5 mm (¼ inch) thick all over.

3 Lightly coat a veal piece with the flour, then dip it into the beaten egg, allowing any excess to drip off. Finally, coat in the breadcrumbs, pressing with your fingertips so that they stick to the veal evenly. Place on a plate and repeat with the remaining veal pieces. Refrigerate for 15 minutes. Preheat the oven to 150°C (300°F/Gas 2).

4 Meanwhile, cook the potatoes in a saucepan of boiling water until tender. Drain. Combine the sour cream, lemon juice, parsley and sugar and stir until smooth; season with salt and black pepper. Add to the potatoes and toss to combine. Set aside and keep warm.

5 Heat half of the oil in a non-stick frying pan over medium–high heat and cook two of the schnitzels for 1–2 minutes on each side, or until golden. Remove to a plate lined with paper towels, then place in the oven to keep warm while cooking the remaining schnitzels with the remaining oil.

6 Serve the schnitzels with the warm potato salad and lemon wedges. It also tastes great served with steamed broccoli.

# lasagne

**ITALY**  Lasagne is one of those dishes that varies greatly, depending on the region. This recipe is based on 'lasagne bolognese' from the town of Bologna in northern Italy. Traditionally béchamel sauce, nutmeg and parmesan are used, usually with pork mince combined with either veal or beef.

375g (13 oz) fresh or 200 g (7 oz) dried lasagne sheets

100 g (3½ oz/1 cup) grated parmesan cheese

**meat sauce**

2 tablespoons olive oil

1 brown onion, finely chopped

100 g (3½ oz) pancetta, finely chopped

1 carrot, finely chopped

1 celery stick, finely chopped

1 kg (2 lb 4 oz) minced (ground) veal and pork

3 garlic cloves, finely chopped

¼ teaspoon ground nutmeg

1 rosemary sprig, leaves chopped

400 g (14 oz/1⅔ cups) tin chopped tomatoes

125 g (4½ oz/½ cup) tomato paste (concentrated purée)

1 litre (35 fl oz/4 cups) chicken stock

**béchamel sauce**

1 litre (35 fl oz/4 cups) milk

½ white onion, halved

¼ teaspoon ground nutmeg

80 g (2¾ oz) butter

75 g (2¾ oz/½ cup) plain (all-purpose) flour

SERVES 8–10

1  To make the meat sauce, heat the oil in a large saucepan over medium heat. Cook the onion, pancetta, carrot and celery for 10 minutes, or until the vegetables have softened. Increase the heat to high, add the mince and cook for 5 minutes, breaking up the meat with a wooden spoon. Add the garlic, nutmeg and rosemary and cook for 5 minutes or until the meat is browned. Stir in the tomatoes, tomato paste and stock. Bring to the boil, reduce the heat to medium and cook, stirring occasionally, for 1 hour or until reduced by half. Season with black pepper, to taste.

2  To make the béchamel sauce, combine the milk, onion and nutmeg in a saucepan and slowly bring to the boil. Remove from the heat and stand for 10 minutes to allow the flavours to infuse. Strain into a heatproof bowl.

3  Melt the butter in a separate saucepan over medium heat. Stir in the flour and cook for 1 minute, stirring constantly to form a thick paste. Remove from the heat and whisk in the hot milk until well combined. Return to medium heat and stir constantly for 2 minutes, or until the sauce boils and thickens. Set aside.

4  Preheat the oven to 200°C (400°F/Gas 6). Spread one-third of the meat sauce over the base of a 30 x 20 x 4 cm (12 x 8 x 1½ inch) ovenproof dish. Cover with a layer of lasagne sheets. Spread half of the remaining meat sauce over the pasta and then half of the béchamel sauce. Sprinkle with half the parmesan. Continue layering, with the remaining meat sauce, lasagne sheets, béchamel and parmesan.

5  Bake for 25 minutes or until the top is golden and the pasta is tender when pierced with a skewer. Stand for 10 minutes before serving with a green salad.

# vegetable and chickpea tagine

**MOROCCO** A tagine is a North African dish that has been named after a traditional cooking pot and simply means a Moroccan stew. It is often flavoured with different spices, such as turmeric, cinnamon and cayenne pepper, and uses a host of ingredients typical of the region, such as sweet potato and chickpeas, and it is sweetened with raisins.

2 tablespoons olive oil

2 brown onions, halved and sliced

1 teaspoon finely grated fresh ginger

2 celery sticks, sliced

250 g (9 oz) sweet potato, peeled and cut into 2 cm (¾ inch) chunks

1 red capsicum (pepper), seeded, membrane removed and chopped

2 teaspoons ground coriander

1 teaspoon ground turmeric

½ teaspoon ground cinnamon

¼ teaspoon cayenne pepper

1 cinnamon stick

400 g (14 oz/1⅔ cups) tin chopped tomatoes

400 g (14 oz) tin chickpeas, rinsed and drained

60 g (2¼ oz/½ cup) raisins, roughly chopped

2 tablespoons freshly squeezed lemon juice

60 ml (2 fl oz/¼ cup) vegetable stock

150 g (5½ oz) green beans, halved

50 g (1¾ oz/⅓ cup) pine nuts, toasted

100 g (3½ oz/⅔ cup) crumbled feta cheese

Greek-style yoghurt, to serve

SERVES 4

1 Heat the oil in a large saucepan over medium heat. Cook the onions for 5 minutes, or until softened. Add the ginger, celery, sweet potato and capsicum and cook for 3 minutes, stirring occasionally.

2 Add the coriander, turmeric, ground cinnamon, cayenne pepper, cinnamon stick and a pinch of salt and cook, stirring, for 1 minute or until fragrant.

3 Stir in the tomatoes, chickpeas, raisins, lemon juice and stock. Increase the heat to high and bring to the boil, then reduce the heat to low, cover, and simmer for 30 minutes. Add the beans and cook, uncovered, for a further 5 minutes or until the vegetables are tender.

4 Remove the cinnamon stick and serve the tagine immediately, sprinkled with the pine nuts and feta and accompanied by some yoghurt and the couscous.

**Note:** You can use 3 teaspoons of a Moroccan spice blend (available in the spice section of the supermarket) in place of the ground coriander, turmeric, cinnamon, cayenne pepper and cinnamon stick if you want.

# chargrilled vegetable pizzas

**ITALY** The modern pizza was born in Naples, Italy, where in 1870, a pizza-maker created the Margerita pizza (see variation below) in honour of the Italian queen. This pizza represented the colours of the Italian flag: tomatoes (red), mozzarella (white) and basil leaves (green).

2 zucchini (courgettes), cut lengthways into 5 mm (¼ inch) thick slices

2 baby eggplants (aubergines), cut lengthways into 5 mm (¼ inch) thick slices

75 g (2¾ oz/½ cup) grated mozzarella cheese

40 g (1½ oz/¼ cup) crumbled feta cheese

**pizza dough**

250 g (9 oz/1⅔ cups) plain flour

1 teaspoon dried yeast

½ teaspoon salt

185 ml (6 fl oz/¾ cup) lukewarm water

2 tablespoons olive oil

**tomato sauce**

1 tablespoon olive oil

1 brown onion, finely chopped

1 garlic clove, crushed

400 g (14 oz/1⅔ cups) tin chopped tomatoes

1 tablespoon tomato paste (concentrated purée)

1 teaspoon sugar

SERVES 4–6

1  To make the pizza dough, combine the flour, yeast and salt in a large bowl and make a well in the centre. Add the water and 1 tablespoon of the oil and use a wooden spoon and then your hands to mix to a soft, slightly sticky dough. Turn onto a floured surface and knead for 10 minutes, or until the dough is smooth and springs back when you prod it with your finger. Place in a large bowl and cover with plastic wrap. Set aside in a warm, draught-free place for 1 hour or until doubled in size.

2  Meanwhile, to make the tomato sauce, heat the oil in a saucepan over medium heat and cook the onion for 10 minutes, or until softened. Add the garlic and cook for 1 minute. Stir in the tomatoes, tomato paste and sugar. Simmer for 30 minutes or until thick; season with salt and black pepper, to taste. Cool.

3  Chargrill the zucchini and eggplant slices on a hot chargrill plate for 2 minutes each side, or until softened.

4  Preheat the oven to 230°C (450°F/Gas 8). Divide the dough into two portions and use a lightly floured rolling pin to roll out two 28 cm (11¼ inch) circles, about 2 mm (¹⁄₁₆ inch) thick. Place on a pizza or oven tray.

5  Spread each base with 125 ml (4 fl oz/½ cup) of the tomato sauce. Place over the grilled vegetables, top with the cheeses and drizzle with the remaining oil. Bake for 12–15 minutes, or until the bases are cooked through. Cut into slices and serve warm.

## VARIATION

*Margerita pizza:* Spread the pizza bases with the tomato sauce (as above) and top with 150 g (5½ oz/1 cup) grated mozzarella cheese. Drizzle with the remaining oil and cook as above, then top the cooked pizza with ¼ cup torn basil leaves.

# burger

USA The earliest record of a hamburger recipe is from the late 1800s in the *Boston Evening Journal*. The hamburger steak was described as '… beef put twice through a meat grinder and mixed with onion and pepper'. By 1912 the meat patties were served in buns and the burger was described as a hot sandwich accompanied by condiments.

olive oil

100 g (3½ oz) grated cheddar cheese

4 hamburger buns, split

mayonnaise, to serve

4 iceberg lettuce leaves

2 ripe tomatoes, sliced

tomato sauce (ketchup), to serve

4 gherkins (pickles) (optional)

**patties**

500 g (1 lb 2 oz) minced (ground) beef

1 brown onion, coarsely grated

50 g (1¾ oz/½ cup) dry breadcrumbs

1 tablespoon milk

1 egg, lightly beaten

1 tablespoon Worcestershire sauce

2–3 drops Tabasco sauce, or to taste

¼ teaspoon ground nutmeg

1 teaspoon dijon mustard

SERVES 4

1　To make the burger patties, put all the ingredients into a mixing bowl and use your hands to mix until well combined. Divide the mixture into four portions and shape each into a patty with a 10 cm (4 inch) diameter.

2　Heat a little oil in a chargrill pan over medium–high heat. Add the patties and cook for 4 minutes, then turn and cook for 3 minutes. Sprinkle each with the grated cheese and cook for a further 2 minutes or until the patties are cooked through and the cheese has melted.

3　Meanwhile, preheat the grill (broiler) to high. Toast the buns, cut side up, under the grill until golden. Place the bases on serving plates and spread each generously with mayonnaise. Top with lettuce, tomato and the patties. Top with tomato sauce and cover with the bun tops, securing a gherkin on top using a toothpick, if desired.

# butter chicken

**INDIA**  Indian cuisine is famous for its many curries and this butter chicken recipe is by far one of the most popular, originating from the Punjab region. Known as *Murgh Makhani*, the chicken can be marinated first in a spiced yoghurt mixture or follow the recipe below if you're in a hurry.

2 tablespoons peanut oil

1 kg (2 lb 4 oz) boneless, skinless chicken thighs, quartered

60 g (2¼ oz) butter or ghee

2 teaspoons garam masala

2 teaspoons sweet paprika

2 teaspoons ground coriander

1 tablespoon finely chopped fresh ginger

¼ teaspoon chilli powder

1 cinnamon stick

6 cardamom pods, bruised

350 ml (12 fl oz oz) tomato passata (puréed tomatoes)

1 tablespoon sugar

60 g (2¼ oz/¼ cup) plain yoghurt

125 ml (4 fl oz/½ cup) pouring (whipping) cream

1 tablespoon freshly squeezed lemon juice

coriander (cilantro) leaves, to serve

**SERVES 4–6**

1  Heat 1 tablespoon of the oil in a wok over high heat and swirl to coat the base and side. Add half of the chicken and stir-fry for 4 minutes, or until browned. Remove to a plate. Repeat with the remaining oil and chicken until it is all cooked. Set aside.

2  Heat the butter in the same wok over low heat. Once the butter has melted, add the garam masala, paprika, ground coriander, ginger, chilli powder, cinnamon stick and cardamom pods and cook for 1 minute, or until fragrant. Return the chicken to the wok and mix well to coat in the spices.

3  Add the tomato passata and sugar and bring to a simmer. Simmer gently for 15 minutes, or until the chicken is tender and the sauce has thickened.

4  Add the yoghurt, cream and lemon juice to the wok and simmer for 5 minutes, or until the sauce has thickened slightly. Garnish with the coriander leaves and serve the butter chicken with steamed rice and poppadoms.

# sides and salads

# cornbread

**USA** European settlers in the United States were first introduced to cornmeal by the Native Americans, who had been grinding corn and cooking it in breads, soups and porridges for many years. This recipe was first developed by Europeans who were trying to cook bread without any access to wheat or yeast. It became very popular as it was cheap to make and stored well. Polenta is a fine yellow cornmeal and it is used in this cornbread recipe.

150 g (5½ oz/1 cup) self-raising flour

150 g (5½ oz/1 cup) fine polenta

1 teaspoon salt

1 egg

250 ml (9 fl oz/1 cup) buttermilk

60 ml (2 fl oz/¼ cup) vegetable oil

butter, to serve (optional)

MAKES 4

1 Preheat the oven to 220°C (425°F/Gas 7). Generously grease four 185 ml (6 fl oz/¾ cup) dariole moulds (ramekins) or muffin holes.

2 Sift the flour into a bowl, add the polenta and salt and make a well in the centre. Whisk together the egg, buttermilk and oil in a separate bowl, then add to the dry ingredients and stir until just combined, being careful not to overmix.

3 Pour the batter into the moulds or muffin holes and bake for about 12–15 minutes, or until the bread is golden brown and a skewer inserted into the centre comes out clean. Serve, warm or at room temperature spread with butter, if desired.

**Note:** If you prefer you can cook one large cornbread in a greased and lined round 20 cm (8 inch) cake tin for 25 minutes. Serve cut into wedges.

# naan

**INDIA**  Although the word naan can be traced back to Persia (now Iran) it is most often associated with Indian cuisine and refers to the leavened, oven-baked flat bread that can be flavoured with garlic and other spices and is usually served with curries — try it with the Southern Indian fish curry (see page 96) or Butter chicken (see page 124).

600 g (1 lb 5 oz/4 cups) plain (all-purpose) flour

1 teaspoon baking powder

½ teaspoon bicarbonate of soda (baking soda)

1 teaspoon salt

250 ml (9 fl oz/1 cup) milk

125 g (4½ oz/½ cup) plain yoghurt

1 egg, beaten

80 g (2¾ oz) ghee or butter, melted

**MAKES 8**

1  Sift together the flour, baking powder, bicarbonate of soda and salt into a large bowl and make a well in the centre. In a separate bowl, mix together the milk, yoghurt, egg and 1 tablespoon of the ghee or butter. Add to the dry ingredients and mix with a wooden spoon and then your hands to make a soft dough.

2  Turn the dough out onto a lightly floured surface and knead until soft and pliable. Place in a lightly floured bowl and cover with plastic wrap or a damp cloth. Leave in a warm, draught-free place for 2 hours.

3  Preheat the oven to 200°C (400°F/Gas 6). Lightly grease two large baking trays.

4  Knead the rested dough on a lightly floured surface for 2–3 minutes, or until smooth and pliable. Divide the dough into eight even-sized portions and roll each one into an oval about 10 cm (4 inches) wide and 15 cm (6 inches) long. Brush with water and place, wet side down, on the baking trays. Brush the naan with the remaining melted ghee or butter.

5  Bake for 8–10 minutes, or until golden brown and cooked through. Serve with Indian curries.

## VARIATION

To make garlic naan, crush 6 garlic cloves and sprinkle evenly over the dough prior to baking.

# tabouleh

**LEBANON** This salad of burghul with finely chopped parsley, mint, tomato and spring onion originated in Lebanon, where it was traditionally served in lettuce leaves or on the side of meat dishes. It is now popular all over the world but is most associated with Middle Eastern cuisine.

130 g (4½ oz/¾ cup) burghul (bulgur)

3 ripe tomatoes

1 telegraph (long) cucumber

4 spring onions, sliced

4 cups chopped flat-leaf (Italian) parsley

½ cup chopped mint

**dressing**

80 ml (2½ fl oz/⅓ cup) olive oil

80 ml (2½ fl oz/⅓ cup) freshly squeezed lemon juice

1 teaspoon salt

SERVES 6

1   Place the burghul in a bowl, cover with 500 ml (17 fl oz/ 2 cups) water and leave for 1½ hours to soak.

2   Drain the burghul and squeeze out any excess water with your hands. Spread the burghul out on a clean tea towel (dish towel) or paper towels and leave to dry for about 30 minutes.

3   Meanwhile, cut the tomatoes in half, squeeze gently to remove any excess seeds and cut into 1 cm (½ inch) dice. Cut the cucumber in half lengthways, remove the seeds with a teaspoon and cut the flesh into 1 cm (½ inch) dice. Place the tomato and cucumber in a large bowl.

4   To make the dressing, place the oil, lemon juice and salt in a screw-top jar and shake well to combine.

5   Add the burghul, spring onion, parsley and mint to the tomato and cucumber and toss well to combine. Pour the dressing over the salad and toss to combine evenly.

# insalata caprese (tomato and bocconcini salad)

**ITALY** The name of this dish literally translates to 'salad in the style of Capri' and refers to the Italian region of Campania. It is always made with mozzarella cheese (or in this case bocconcini), basil and tomatoes and seasoned with olive oil, salt and pepper.

400 g (14 oz) cherry tomatoes, quartered

250 g (9 oz) bocconcini, torn into chunks

¼ cup basil leaves

2 tablespoons olive oil

SERVES 4

1 Combine the tomato, bocconcini and basil on serving plates or in a bowl.

2 Drizzle with the oil and season well with salt and black pepper.

**Note:** You could use whole cherry tomatoes and cut the bocconcini into thin slices if you prefer.

# greek salad

**GREECE** This popular salad makes a great side dish, and although the ingredients may vary slightly, a recipe for Greek salad will almost always use the most favoured ingredients of the cuisine, including olives, feta cheese, tomato, cucumber, lemon juice and olive oil.

1 green capsicum (pepper)

150 g (5½ oz) Greek feta cheese

2 large tomatoes, cut into wedges

1 Lebanese (short) cucumber, sliced

1 small red onion, thinly sliced (optional)

60 g (2¼ oz/⅓ cup) kalamata olives

2 tablespoons freshly squeezed lemon juice

60 ml (2 fl oz/¼ cup) olive oil

SERVES 4

1 Cut the capsicum in half lengthways and remove the seeds and membrane. Cut the flesh into small squares.

2 Cut the feta cheese into small cubes.

3 Combine the capsicum, cheese, tomato, cucumber, onion, if using, and olives in a large bowl. Drizzle with the lemon juice and oil. Season with salt and black pepper, to taste. Toss gently to combine.

# pilaf

**MIDDLE EAST** Pilaf is a common rice dish found on tables throughout the entire Middle East. There are hundreds of varieties of pilafs from Syria to Turkey to Greece — and they vary by culture, ingredients and the meat dish that it is served with.

300 g (10½ oz/1½ cups) basmati rice, washed

2 tablespoons olive oil

2 tablespoons butter

1 brown onion, finely diced

1 tablespoon ground cumin

2 teaspoons ground ginger

1 teaspoon ground turmeric

100 g (3½ oz) angel hair pasta, cut into 2 cm (¾ inch) lengths

625 ml (21½ fl oz/2½ cups) chicken stock

¼ cup chopped flat-leaf (Italian) parsley

90 g (3¼ oz/1 cup) flaked almonds, toasted

**SERVES 6**

1   Rinse the rice under cold running water until the water runs clear.

2   Heat 1 tablespoon of the oil and 1 tablespoon of the butter in a saucepan over medium heat. When the butter foams, add the onion and cook for 5 minutes, or until softened. Add the cumin, ginger and turmeric and cook for 1 minute, or until fragrant.

3   Meanwhile, heat the remaining oil and butter in a frying pan over medium–high heat. Add the pasta and cook, stirring, for 5 minutes, or until golden.

4   Add the rice and browned pasta to the saucepan with the onion mixture and stir to coat. Stir in the stock and 60 ml (2 fl oz/¼ cup) water and bring to the boil over high heat. Reduce the heat to low, cover, and simmer for 12 minutes, or until the rice and pasta are tender — steam holes will appear on the surface of the rice and all the stock will have been absorbed. Remove from the heat and set aside, covered, for 5 minutes.

5   Use a fork to gently stir the parsley and almonds through the rice mixture. Serve warm.

# dhal

INDIA Lentils made their way to India in the 1st century, where they have been used to make this traditional dish for hundreds of years. Serve it with Indian curries and naan bread.

200 g (7 oz) red lentils

5 cm (2 inch) piece fresh ginger, cut into 3 slices

½ teaspoon ground turmeric

½ teaspoon salt

1 tablespoon ghee or oil

1 brown onion, finely chopped

½ teaspoon yellow mustard seeds

2 garlic cloves, crushed

1 teaspoon cumin seeds

1 teaspoon ground coriander

2 fresh green chillies, halved lengthways

2 tablespoons freshly squeezed lemon juice

1 tablespoon chopped coriander (cilantro) leaves

SERVES 4–6

1 Put the lentils and 750 ml (26 fl oz/3 cups) water in a saucepan and bring to the boil. Reduce the heat, add the ginger and turmeric, cover, and simmer for 20 minutes, stirring occasionally to prevent sticking, until the lentils are tender. Remove and discard the ginger slices and stir in the salt.

2 Meanwhile, heat the ghee or oil in a frying pan over medium–high heat. Cook the onion and mustard seeds for 5 minutes, or until the onion is golden. Reduce the heat to medium, add the garlic, cumin, ground coriander and chilli and cook for 2 minutes, or until fragrant.

3 Add the onion mixture to the lentils and stir gently. Add 125 ml (4 fl oz/½ cup) water, place over low heat and cook for 5 minutes. Stir in the lemon juice and serve sprinkled with the coriander.

# roasted vegetables

ENGLAND Vegetables have a long tradition of being added to the roasting tin with meats. The vegetables can be flavoured with a variety of herbs, here we have used rosemary.

6 all-purpose potatoes, peeled and halved

400 g (14 oz) kent pumpkin (winter squash) unpeeled, cut into thick wedges

4 small parsnips, peeled, trimmed and halved lengthways

2 large red onions, quartered

80 ml (2½ fl oz/⅓ cup) olive oil

2 tablespoons chopped rosemary leaves

SERVES 4

1 Preheat the oven to 200°C (400°F/Gas 6). Put all of the vegetables, with the oil and rosemary in a large bowl. Season well with salt and black pepper and toss well to combine.

2 Put the vegetables in a roasting tin in a single layer. Roast, turning once, for 45 minutes, or until the vegetables are tender and golden. Serve warm.

# ratatouille (vegetable stew)

**FRANCE** Ratatouille comes from the French term 'touiller', which means to toss food. It started as a peasant dish in Nice, and was prepared by farmers to use up excess summer vegetables.

100 ml (3½ fl oz) olive oil

500 g (1 lb 2 oz) eggplants (aubergines), cut into 2 cm (¾ inch) chunks

375 g (13 oz) zucchini (courgettes), thickly sliced

1 green capsicum (pepper), seeded, membrane removed and cut into 2 cm (¾ inch) pieces

1 red onion, cut into wedges

3 garlic cloves, finely chopped

2 teaspoons chopped thyme leaves

2 bay leaves

6 vine-ripened tomatoes, peeled and chopped

1 tablespoon red wine vinegar

1 teaspoon caster (superfine) sugar

¼ cup shredded basil leaves

SERVES 4–6

1   Heat 2 tablespoons of the oil in a large saucepan over medium heat. Cook the eggplant, in batches, for 5 minutes, or until softened. Remove and set aside. Heat another 2 tablespoons of the oil in the pan, add the zucchini and cook for 4 minutes, or until softened. Remove and set aside. Add the capsicum and cook for 2 minutes, or until starting to soften. Remove and set aside.

2   Heat the remaining oil in the pan and cook the onion for 5 minutes, or until softened. Add the garlic, thyme and bay leaves, and cook, stirring, for 1 minute or until fragrant. Return the eggplant, zucchini and capsicum to the pan and add the tomato, vinegar and sugar. Simmer for 20 minutes, or until the vegetables are tender. Stir in the basil and season with salt and black pepper. Serve warm.

# zucchini and haloumi fritters

**GREECE**  These fritters are made with a traditional Middle Eastern cheese called haloumi. They are great served with chargrilled meats and make a good snack or lunch.

300 g (10½ oz) zucchini (courgettes)

4 spring onions (scallions), thinly sliced

200 g (7 oz) haloumi cheese, coarsely grated (see note)

40 g (1½ oz/¼ cup) plain (all-purpose) flour

2 eggs

1 tablespoon chopped dill

60 ml (2 fl oz/¼ cup) vegetable oil

Greek-style yoghurt and lemon wedges, to serve

**MAKES 16 (SERVES 4–6)**

1  Preheat the oven to 120°C (235°F/Gas ½).

2  Coarsely grate the zucchini then, using your hands, squeeze out as much liquid as possible. Put the zucchini in a large bowl with the spring onion, haloumi, flour, eggs and dill. Season well with salt and black pepper and mix until evenly combined.

3  Heat the oil in a large heavy–based frying pan over medium–high heat. Drop tablespoonfuls of the mixture into the pan and cook, in batches, for 2 minutes each side, or until golden and cooked through. Drain on paper towels, then transfer to a baking tray and keep warm in the oven while cooking the remaining fritters.

4  Serve the fritters immediately with the yoghurt and lemon wedges.

**Note:** The fritters are best prepared and cooked as close to the serving time as possible, or the haloumi will become tough as it cools.

# something sweet

# pavlova

**AUSTRALIA** The exact origin of this dessert is hotly debated between Australians and New Zealanders — both claiming it as their own. It is named after a famous Russian ballerina, Anna Pavlova, who toured both countries in the 1920s, to honour her light and airy dancing style.

4 egg whites

220 g (7¾ oz/1 cup) caster (superfine) sugar

1 tablespoon cornflour (cornstarch), sifted

375 ml (13 fl oz/1½ cups) thickened (whipping) cream

2 tablespoons icing (confectioners') sugar

2 small bananas, sliced

250 g (9 oz/1⅔ cups) strawberries, hulled and halved

2 passionfruit, halved

SERVES 6–8

1 Preheat the oven to 130°C (250°F/Gas 1). Line a baking tray with baking paper. Draw a 20 cm (8 inch) circle on the paper and then turn the paper over.

2 Using electric beaters, whisk the egg whites in a large, dry bowl until soft peaks form. Gradually add the caster sugar, whisking well after each addition. Continue whisking until the mixture is very thick and glossy and the sugar has completely dissolved. Test by rubbing a small amount of the mixture between your thumb and forefinger — it should feel smooth and not gritty. If it feels gritty, continue whisking for a few more minutes. Use a large metal spoon to fold in the cornflour.

3 Use the back of a spoon to spread the meringue mixture onto the tray, using the marked circle as a guide and making a shallow well in the centre. Bake for 1½ hours. Leave to cool in the oven with the door ajar.

4 Using electric beaters, whisk the cream and icing sugar until soft peaks form.

5 Spread the pavlova with cream, pile on the banana and strawberries and scrape over the passionfruit pulp.

# crème caramel

**FRANCE** Also called a French flan, crème caramel is a silky smooth cooked custard that, when turned out of its dish, is coated with a delicious caramel sauce. Variations of this dessert also exist in other countries such as Spain, Mexico and Portugal.

melted butter, for brushing

165 g (5¾ oz/¾ cup) sugar

**custard**

750 ml (26 fl oz/3 cups) milk

75 g (2¾ oz/⅓ cup) caster (superfine) sugar

4 eggs

1 teaspoon natural vanilla extract

SERVES 8

1  Preheat the oven to 160°C (315°F/Gas 2–3). Brush eight 125 ml (4 fl oz/½ cup) ramekins or dariole moulds with melted butter.

2  Place the sugar and 60 ml (2 fl oz/¼ cup) water in a small saucepan. Stir over low heat until the sugar dissolves. Bring to the boil, reduce the heat and simmer, without stirring, until the mixture turns a deep golden colour. Occasionally, brush down the side of the pan with a pastry brush dipped in water. Remove from the heat and carefully pour the hot caramel into the ramekins to cover the bases. Place the ramekins into a baking dish.

3  To make the custard, put the milk in a saucepan and bring almost to the boil over medium heat. Remove from the heat. Use a balloon whisk to whisk together the caster sugar, eggs and vanilla until thick. Use the whisk to stir the egg mixture into the warm milk. Strain the mixture into a bowl and pour into the ramekins.

4  Add enough boiling water to the baking dish to come halfway up the sides of the ramekins. Bake for 30 minutes, or until the custard is just set. The custards should be no longer liquid but should wobble slightly when the ramekins are shaken lightly. Remove from the water and cool, then refrigerate for at least 2 hours, or until set.

5  To unmould, run a knife carefully around the edge of each custard and gently turn out onto serving plates. Shake gently to help them come out, if necessary. Serve with mixed berries.

# individual summer puddings

**ENGLAND** The British claim this sweet pudding as their own. The name comes from the use of summer berries, usually a mixture of blackberries, black currants, raspberries and red currants, although you can use any combination you prefer.

1 kg (2 lb 4 oz) frozen mixed berries

75 g (2¾ oz/⅓ cup) caster (superfine) sugar, or to taste

18 slices good-quality white bread, crusts removed

whipped cream, to serve (optional)

SERVES 6

1 Put the berries in a saucepan with 125 ml (4 fl oz/ ½ cup) water and heat gently until the berries begin to collapse. Turn off the heat and stir in the sugar. Set aside to cool. Strain the berries, reserving the juice.

2 Using a round cutter, cut out six rounds of the bread slices to line the base of six 150 ml (5 fl oz) ramekins or dariole moulds. Cut the bread into strips to fit the sides.

3 Lightly press the bread into the moulds to line, leaving no gaps. Drizzle about 1 tablespoon of the reserved berry juice over the bread in each mould. Then add the berries and add another 2 tablespoons of the reserved juice to each. Use a cutter to cut out six rounds of bread to cover the puddings. Reserve any remaining berries and juice.

4 Cover the puddings with plastic wrap. Place a saucer with a weight (such as a tin of tomatoes) on the top of each pudding. Refrigerate overnight.

5 Carefully turn out the puddings and serve with cream, if desired, and the remaining berries and juice.

# crepes with lemon and sugar

**FRANCE** Crepes are considered to be one of the French national dishes and originated in the northwest, in Brittany. The word is from the Latin meaning *crispa* or 'curled', referring to their thin texture and the way the edges appear slightly curled when perfectly cooked.

150 g (5½ oz/1 cup) plain (all–purpose) flour

4 eggs

500 ml (17 fl oz/2 cups) milk

melted butter, for brushing

sugar, for sprinkling

lemon juice, for sprinkling

lemon wedges, to serve

MAKES 12

1  Place the flour in a bowl. In a separate bowl, whisk together the eggs and milk. Gradually add to the flour, whisking constantly until smooth. Transfer to a jug, cover with plastic wrap and set aside for 30 minutes.

2  Meanwhile, preheat the oven to 120°C (235°F/Gas ½).

3  Lightly brush a 20 cm (8 inch) non-stick crepe pan or frying pan with melted butter. Pour 60 ml (2 fl oz/¼ cup) of batter into the pan at a time and swirl to coat the base. Cook for 1 minute, or until golden underneath, then turn and cook the other side for 30 seconds. Remove to a plate, cover with foil, and keep warm in the oven. Repeat with the remaining batter.

4  Sprinkle each crepe with sugar and drizzle with a little lemon juice before folding in triangles. Serve with lemon wedges on the side to squeeze over.

# cardamom rice pudding

**INDIA** Also known as *kheer* in India (derived from a sanskrit word meaning 'milk'), this is one of the nation's most popular desserts — a creamy rice pudding flavoured with a hint of cardamom spice, flaked almonds and sultanas. Yum!

6 cardamom pods

150 g (5½ oz/¾ cup) basmati rice

110 g (3¾ oz/½ cup) sugar

1 litre (35 fl oz/4 cups) milk

30 g (1 oz/⅓ cup) flaked almonds, toasted

30 g (1 oz/¼ cup) sultanas (golden raisins)

SERVES 8

1　Lightly crush the cardamom pods using a rolling pin or a mortar and pestle. Place in a medium saucepan.

2　Add the rice, sugar and milk to the pan and bring to the boil over medium–high heat. Reduce the heat to low and simmer gently for 35 minutes, or until the rice is tender and the mixture is very creamy, stirring occasionally with a spoon to prevent the rice from sticking to the pan.

3　Reserve a few of the almonds and sultanas for garnish, then add the remainder to the rice mixture and stir to combine evenly. Divide among bowls and serve warm, garnished with the reserved almonds and sultanas.

# tiramisu

**ITALY** This traditional dessert is made using sponge finger biscuits dipped in hot coffee (we use chocolate instead) and layered in a mixture of egg yolks and mascarpone cheese with a hint of cocoa. The name means 'carry me up' — is it to heaven? It must be somewhere close!

5 eggs, separated

165 g (5¾ oz/¾ cup) caster (superfine) sugar

300 g (10½ oz/1⅓ cups) mascarpone cheese

40 g (1½ oz/⅓ cup) drinking chocolate

500 ml (17 fl oz/2 cups) boiling water

44 small savoiardi (lady fingers/ sponge finger biscuits)

90 g (3¼ oz/¾ cup) finely grated dark chocolate

SERVES 6

1. Using electric beaters, whisk the egg yolks with the sugar in a bowl until the mixture is thick and pale and leaves a ribbon trail when the beaters are lifted. Add the mascarpone and whisk briefly until just smooth (don't overmix or the mixture will separate).

2. Using clean, dry beaters and bowl, whisk the egg whites until soft peaks form, then fold them into the mascarpone mixture.

3. Combine the drinking chocolate and 80 ml (2½ fl oz/ ⅓ cup) of the boiling water and mix to a smooth paste. Gradually stir in the remaining boiling water. Transfer to a shallow dish and cool slightly. Dip half the biscuits into the chocolate mixture for 2–3 seconds; the biscuits should be well soaked but not breaking up. Arrange the biscuits snugly in the base of a lined 20 cm (8 inch) square dish or cake tin.

4. Spread half the mascarpone mixture over the biscuits, smoothing the surface. Dip the remaining biscuits into the chocolate mixture and use these to neatly cover the mascarpone layer, then top with the remaining mascarpone mixture, smoothing the surface. Cover the dish with plastic wrap and refrigerate for 3 hours or overnight. Sprinkle with the grated chocolate, then cut into portions or spoon into bowls.

# hot chocolate soufflés

**FRANCE**  There are many different types of soufflés, both savoury and sweet. This dessert takes its name from the French verb *souffler*, which means 'to blow up', and is a good description of how it magically inflates during cooking, thanks to the addition of fluffy egg whites.

melted butter, for greasing

145 g (5½ oz/⅔ cup) caster (superfine) sugar

30g (1 oz) unsalted butter, cubed

2 tablespoons plain (all-purpose) flour

500 ml (17 fl oz/2 cups) milk

2 eggs, at room temperature, separated

150 g (5½ oz/1 cup) finely chopped dark chocolate

thick (double/heavy) cream, to serve

**SERVES 6**

1  Line a baking tray with baking paper. Grease six 185 ml (6 fl oz/¾ cup) soufflé dishes or ramekins with melted butter. Use 1½ tablespoons of the caster sugar to coat the insides of the dishes. Place on the prepared tray.

2  Melt the butter in a small saucepan over medium heat. Stir in the flour and cook for 1 minute, or until bubbling. Use a balloon whisk to gradually stir in the milk until smooth. Cook over medium heat, stirring constantly, until the custard thickens and boils, then reduce the heat and simmer for 1 minute.

3  Transfer the custard to a large heatproof bowl and stir in half the remaining caster sugar, with the egg yolks and chocolate until the chocolate melts and the mixture is smooth. Cover the surface of the chocolate custard with plastic wrap and refrigerate for 30 minutes, stirring occasionally, until cooled to room temperature.

4  Preheat the oven to 190°C (375°F/Gas 5). Use electric beaters with a whisk attachment to whisk the egg whites until soft peaks form. Gradually whisk in the remaining sugar. Use a large metal spoon or spatula to fold half the egg whites into the chocolate custard. Fold in the remaining egg whites until just combined.

5  Divide the mixture evenly among the prepared dishes and use the back of a spoon to carefully smooth the surfaces. Cook in the oven for 35 minutes, or until well risen. Serve immediately with the cream on the side.

# strawberry shortcakes

USA  Strawberry shortcake is a classic American dish. It is usually made as a round of scone-like shortcake which is split, then filled or topped with fresh strawberries to make this terrifically sweet treat. Here we use a delicious shortbread pastry to sandwich the filling.

## shortbread

150 g (5½ oz/1 cup) plain (all-purpose) flour

2 tablespoons cornflour (cornstarch)

125 g (4½ oz) butter, at room temperature

55 g (2 oz/¼ cup) sugar

## filling

300 ml (10½ fl oz) thickened (whipping)cream

1 tablespoon icing (confectioners') sugar, plus extra, to dust

250 g (9 oz/1⅔ cups) strawberries, hulled and quartered

SERVES 4

1  Sift the flour and cornflour into a bowl. Use electric beaters to beat the butter and sugar in a separate bowl until just combined. Add the flour and use a wooden spoon and then your hands to mix to a soft pastry. Turn onto a lightly floured surface and shape into a disc. Wrap in plastic wrap and refrigerate for 30 minutes.

2  Preheat the oven to 160°C (315°F/Gas 2–3). Line two baking trays with baking paper.

3  Use a lightly floured rolling pin to roll out half the pastry to about 8 mm (⅜ inch) thick. Use a large heart-shaped cutter to cut out four biscuits, re-rolling the pastry if necessary. Place on the oven trays. Repeat with the remaining pastry. Refrigerate for a further 20 minutes.

4  Bake in the oven for 20 minutes, or until golden and cooked through. Allow to cool on the trays.

5  To serve, whisk the cream with the icing sugar until soft peaks form. Place half the shortbread hearts on serving plates and top each with some cream, strawberries and another shortbread heart. Dust with icing sugar.

# sago pudding

**MALAYSIA** Sago is a starch extracted from Southeast Asian palms and processed into tiny balls known as pearl sago; it is often used to make milk-based puddings. In this Malay dessert, also called *gula melaka*, the sago gives it a truly unique texture.

195 g (7 oz/1 cup) pearl sago

230 g (8½ oz/1¼ cups) lightly packed
soft brown sugar

250 ml (9 fl oz/1 cup) coconut cream, chilled

SERVES 6

1 Soak the sago in 750 ml (26 fl oz/3 cups) water for 1 hour.

2 Put the sago and water into a saucepan and stir in 2 tablespoons of the brown sugar. Bring to the boil over low heat, stirring constantly.

3 Reduce the heat and simmer, stirring occasionally, for 10 minutes. Cover and cook over low heat, stirring occasionally, for 2–3 minutes, until the mixture is thick and the sago grains are translucent.

4 Divide the sago mixture among six rinsed (still wet) 125 ml (4 fl oz/½ cup) ramekins or dariole moulds. Cover and refrigerate for 2 hours, or until set.

5 Combine the remaining brown sugar with 60 ml (2 fl oz/¼ cup) water in a small saucepan and stir over low heat until the sugar dissolves. Bring to the boil and simmer for 5 minutes or until the syrup thickens slightly. Pour into a heatproof jug and cool.

6 To serve, unmould the sago puddings into bowls. Serve with a little coconut cream and the brown sugar syrup.

# strawberry granita

**ITALY** Granita hails from the Italian island of Sicily. Unlike gelato, it is based on water, not milk. Once frozen the ice crystals are then broken up by scraping them with a fork to make a refreshing icy dessert. Traditionally it is made with coffee or lemon, but this strawberry version is delicious!

125 g (4½ oz) sugar

500 g (1 lb 2 oz/3⅓ cups) strawberries, hulled

2 tablespoons freshly squeezed lemon juice

thick (double/heavy) cream, to serve (optional)

**SERVES 4**

1 Put the sugar and 125 ml (4 fl oz/½ cup) water in a saucepan and stir over low heat until the sugar has dissolved. Bring to the boil and simmer for 5 minutes. Leave to cool.

2 Purée the strawberries with the lemon juice in a food processor or blender until smooth. Add the cooled sugar syrup and process to combine. Pass the mixture through a sieve.

3 Pour the mixture into a shallow metal container, cover, and freeze for 2 hours, or until frozen around the edge of the tray. Stir with a fork to break up the ice crystals. Return to the freezer for 1 hour and stir again with a fork. Repeat this until the mixture is a smooth consistency of ice crystals, then transfer to an airtight container. Return to the freezer for 3–4 hours, or until set.

4 To serve, soften the frozen mixture in the refrigerator for 15–20 minutes. Scrape the granita with a fork to break up the ice crystals and then spoon into serving dishes. Serve with a dollop of cream, if desired.

**Note:** If you have stored the granita for a few days, you may need to fork and freeze it again more than once until you get it to the correct consistency for serving.

# petits pots au chocolat

**FRANCE** These 'little chocolate pots' are a typical French custard-like dessert, made with milk, cream and chocolate and then baked in a bain-marie or 'water bath' to create a velvety smooth pudding texture that you won't be able to resist. *Bon appetit!*

150 g (5½ oz/1 cup) good-quality chopped dark chocolate

170 g (6 oz/¾ cup) thick (double/heavy) cream

80 ml (2½ fl oz/⅓ cup) milk

2 egg yolks

55 g (2 oz/¼ cup) caster (superfine) sugar

1 teaspoon natural vanilla extract

SERVES 8

1   Lightly brush eight 80 ml (2½ fl oz/⅓ cup) ovenproof dariole moulds or ramekins with melted butter and put them in a deep baking dish. Preheat the oven to 140°C (275°F/Gas 1).

2   Combine the chocolate, cream and milk in a small saucepan. Stir constantly over low heat until the chocolate has just melted.

3   Place the egg yolks in a small bowl and gradually whisk in the sugar with a balloon whisk. Continue whisking until the sugar has dissolved and the mixture is pale and creamy. Add the melted chocolate mixture and vanilla and whisk until well combined. Pour into the moulds. Fill the baking dish with enough boiling water to come halfway up the sides of the moulds. Bake for 45 minutes, or until set.

4   Carefully remove the baking dish from the oven and cool the *Petits pots au chocolat* completely in the water bath. When cool, remove the moulds from the water bath, cover with plastic wrap and refrigerate for 6 hours.

5   To serve, top with a dollop of cream and dust with cocoa powder.

# linzertorte

**AUSTRIA** Arguably the oldest cake in the world (the word *torte* is German for 'cake'), the Linzertorte is from the town of Linz in Austria. It always uses ground almonds in the pastry, has a lattice pattern on top, and is filled with jam (traditionally, red currant jam).

315 g (11 oz/1 cup) raspberry jam

1 egg yolk

80 g (2¾ oz/¼ cup) apricot jam

**pastry**

225 g (8 oz/1½ cups) plain (all-purpose) flour

½ teaspoon ground cinnamon

90 g (3¼ oz) unsalted butter, chilled, cubed

55 g (2 oz/¼ cup) caster (superfine) sugar

100 g (3½ oz/1 cup) ground almonds

1 egg yolk, lightly beaten

2 tablespoons freshly squeezed lemon juice or water

SERVES 8

1  To make the pastry, put the flour and cinnamon in a bowl and rub in the butter with your fingertips until the mixture resembles fine breadcrumbs. Stir in the sugar and ground almonds. Make a well in the centre and add the egg yolk and lemon juice. Mix with a flat-bladed knife, using a cutting action, until the mixture just comes together, adding a little more lemon juice if needed. Turn out onto a lightly floured surface and knead briefly until smooth. Shape into a disc, wrap in plastic wrap, and chill for 20 minutes to rest.

2  Roll two-thirds of the pastry out between two sheets of baking paper into a 20 cm (8 inch) circle, about 3 mm (⅛ inch) thick. Use the pastry to line a fluted flan (tart) tin with a removable base. Press the pastry gently into the tin and trim away any excess pastry by rolling the rolling pin over the top. Spread the raspberry jam over the base of the flan.

3  Roll out the remaining pastry, including any scraps, on a lightly floured surface until 3 mm (⅛ inch) thick. Cut it into 2 cm (¾ inch) strips with a fluted pastry wheel or sharp knife. Lay half the strips on a sheet of baking paper, leaving a 2 cm (¾ inch) gap between each strip. Interweave the remaining strips to form a lattice pattern. Carefully transfer to the top of the flan and trim the edges. Place the flan tin on a baking tray, cover with plastic wrap and refrigerate for 20 minutes.

4  Preheat the oven to 180°C (350°F/Gas 4). Combine the remaining egg yolk with 1 teaspoon water and brush lightly over the flan. Bake for 25–30 minutes, or until the pastry is golden brown and cooked through.

5  Meanwhile, heat the apricot jam with 1 tablespoon water, then strain. Brush the warm jam over the flan while hot. Leave to cool in the tin. Serve cut into wedges.

# new york cheesecake

**USA** Almost everyone has tasted a variety of this delicious cheesecake, which gained much popularity in New York City. It uses a lot of cream cheese, which gives it a creamy, but wickedly rich texture — a dessert that anyone would be very happy to be served.

### base

250 g (9 oz) plain sweet biscuits (cookies)

125 g (4½ oz) butter, melted

### filling

750 g (1 lb 10 oz/3 cups) cream cheese, softened

220 g (7¾ oz/1 cup) caster (superfine) sugar

35 g (1¼ oz/¼ cup) plain (all-purpose) flour

2 teaspoons finely grated orange zest

2 teaspoons finely grated lemon zest

4 eggs

185 ml (6 fl oz/¾ cup) pouring (whipping) cream

**SERVES 12**

1   Preheat the oven to 150°C (300°F/Gas 2). Grease a 22 cm (8½ inch) round spring-form cake tin.

2   To make the base, process the biscuits in a food processor until finely crushed. Add the melted butter and process until just combined. Press the biscuit mixture evenly over the base and side of the tin, reaching about three-quarters of the way up. Refrigerate while making the filling.

3   To make the filling, use electric beaters to beat the cream cheese, sugar, flour and orange and lemon zests together in a bowl until smooth. Add the eggs, one at a time, beating well after each addition. Beat in the cream until just combined. Pour the filling into the tin over the base and tap lightly on the bench to settle the mixture.

4   Bake in the oven for 1 hour 25 minutes, or until just set in the centre. Cool in the tin on a wire rack. Refrigerate for at least 3 hours before serving.

5   Remove the cheesecake from the tin and serve in wedges with mixed berries.

# scottish shortbread

**SCOTLAND** Shortbread evolved from a medieval Scottish recipe and was labelled as a bread by bakers who wanted to avoid paying the tax on biscuits. This style of shortbread, known as petticoat tails, a favourite of Mary Queen of Scots, resembled the triangular fabric pieces used in the day to make petticoats that the ladies wore.

250 g (9 oz) unsalted butter, softened

125 g (4½ oz) caster (superfine) sugar

300 g (10½ oz/2 cups) plain (all-purpose) flour

115 g (4 oz/⅔ cup) rice flour

sugar, to sprinkle

**MAKES 16 PIECES**

1 Preheat the oven to 160°C (315°F/Gas 2–3). Mark a 20 cm (8 inch) circle on two pieces of baking paper, then turn the paper over.

2 Beat the butter and caster sugar in a small bowl with electric beaters until light and fluffy. Add the sifted flours and a pinch of salt and mix with a knife, using a cutting action, to form a soft dough. Gather together with your fingertips and divide into two even-sized portions. Shape each portion into a disc and wrap in plastic wrap. Refrigerate for 20 minutes.

3 Use a lightly floured rolling pin to roll out the dough on the baking paper to fit the 20 cm (8 inch) rounds. Neaten the edges then pinch them decoratively. Place each round, still on the paper, onto an oven tray. Use a sharp knife to mark each round into eight wedges. Prick the surface with a fork and sprinkle with sugar.

4 Bake for 35 minutes or until firm, pale golden and cooked through. Cool on the trays. Cut into wedges and store in an airtight container.

**Note:** This shortbread can be stored in an airtight container for up to 1 week.

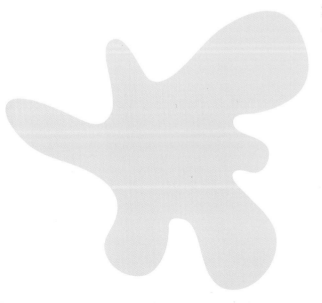

# portuguese custard tarts

**PORTUGAL** It is said the recipe of these egg custard tarts was kept secret for over 300 years by monks living in Lisbon, Portugal. Due to political upheaval in the 1830s the monks had to flee the monastery and, lucky for us, the legendary secret recipe filtered throughout the country.

### pastry

185 g (6½ oz/1¼ cups) plain (all-purpose) flour

25 g (1 oz) Copha (white vegetable shortening), chopped and softened

30 g (1 oz) unsalted butter, softened

### filling

220 g (7¾ oz/1 cup) sugar

30 g (1 oz/¼ cup) cornflour (cornstarch)

1 tablespoon custard powder

500 ml (17 fl oz/2 cups) milk

4 egg yolks, lightly whisked

1 teaspoon natural vanilla extract

MAKES 12

1  To make the pastry, sift the flour into a large bowl and gradually add 170 ml (5½ fl oz/⅔ cup) water, or enough to form a soft dough. Gather the dough into a ball, then roll out between two large sheets of baking paper to form a 24 x 30 cm (9½ x 12 inch) rectangle. Spread the Copha over the surface. Roll up from the short edge to form a log.

2  Roll the dough out into a rectangle again and spread with the butter. Roll up again into a roll and cut into 12 even slices. Place each pastry slice in the base of a muffin tin with 80 ml (2½ floz/⅓ cup) holes. Working from the centre outwards, use your fingertips to press each portion to line the base and side. Refrigerate until needed.

3  To make the filling, put the sugar and 80 ml (2½ fl oz/⅓ cup) water in a small saucepan and stir over low heat until the sugar dissolves. Set aside. Combine the cornflour and custard powder in a small bowl and stir in a little of the milk to form a smooth paste. Add to the pan with the remaining milk, egg yolk and vanilla. Stir over low heat until the mixture thickens. Transfer to a bowl, cover and cool.

4  Preheat the oven to 220°C (425°F/Gas 7).

5  Divide the filling among the pastry cases. Bake for 25–30 minutes, or until the custard is set and the tops have browned. Cool in the tin before serving.

# lamingtons

**AUSTRALIA** An Australian icon, lamingtons are sometimes filled with cream and jam, although traditionally they are just sponge or butter cake squares dipped in chocolate and rolled in coconut. They were named after Lord Lamington, who was the Governor of Queensland from 1896 to 1901.

150 g (5½ oz/1 cup) self-raising flour

75 g (2¾ oz/½ cup) plain (all-purpose) flour

125 g (4½ oz) butter, cubed and softened

145 g (5½ oz/⅔ cup) caster (superfine) sugar

3 eggs, at room temperature

60 ml (2 fl oz/¼ cup) milk

1 teaspoon natural vanilla extract

270 g (9½ oz/3 cups) desiccated coconut

**icing**

500 g (1 lb 2 oz/4 cups) icing (confectioners') sugar

40 g (1½ oz/⅓ cup) unsweetened cocoa powder

30g (1 oz) butter, cubed

125 ml (4 fl oz/½ cup) boiling water

MAKES 16

1 Preheat the oven to 180°C (350°F/Gas 4). Lightly grease a 20 cm (8 inch) square cake tin and line the base and sides with baking paper.

2 Sift the flours into a medium mixing bowl. Add the butter, sugar, eggs, milk and vanilla. Using electric beaters, mix on low speed until the ingredients are just combined. Increase the speed to high and beat for 3–5 minutes, or until free of lumps, pale in colour and increased in volume. Spoon the cake mixture into the tin and smooth the surface with the back of a spoon. Bake for 35–40 minutes, or until a skewer comes out clean when inserted in the centre. Leave in the tin for 5 minutes before turning out onto a wire rack to cool.

3 Using a sharp serrated knife, trim the top of the cooled cake to level it, if necessary. Trim the crusts from the sides and then cut the cake into 16 squares.

4 Place 90 g (3¼ oz/1 cup) of the coconut on a sheet of baking paper or a plate. To make the icing, sift the icing sugar and cocoa into a large bowl. Add the butter to the boiling water and stir until it melts. Add to the icing sugar mixture and stir until smooth. Using two forks, dip a piece of cake in the chocolate icing to coat, then hold the cake over the bowl and allow the excess to drain. (Add a little more boiling water to the icing if it is too thick.) Roll the cake in coconut to coat evenly, then place on a wire rack. Repeat with the remaining cake, adding the remaining coconut as needed.

**Note:** If you cook the cake a day ahead, it will be easier to cut and won't crumble as much when coating in the chocolate icing.

# lebkuchen

**GERMANY**  Lebkuchen was first made in the city of Nuremberg in 1835. It is a spiced biscuit, much like a soft brown ginger cake with a hard white icing. It is popular during the Christmas season all over Germany. Here we have iced the biscuits with delicious white chocolate.

350 g (12 oz/2⅓ cups) plain (all-purpose) flour

60 g (2¼ oz/½ cup) cornflour (cornstarch)

60 g (2¼ oz/⅓ cup) lightly packed brown sugar

1 teaspoon mixed (pumpkin pie) spice

1 teaspoon ground cinnamon

½ teaspoon ground nutmeg

100 g (3½ oz) unsalted butter, cubed

260 g (9¼ oz/¾ cup) golden syrup

2 tablespoons milk

300 g (10½ oz/2 cups) white chocolate melts

**MAKES ABOUT 48**

1  Preheat the oven to 180°C (350°F/Gas 4). Line two large baking trays with baking paper.

2  Sift the flours, sugar and spices into a large bowl and make a well in the centre.

3  Put the butter, golden syrup and milk in a small saucepan over low heat. Stir until the butter has melted and the mixture is smooth. Remove from the heat and stir into the dry ingredients with a wooden spoon until well combined (the mixture will be quite wet). Set aside to cool to room temperature.

4  Divide the dough into three portions. Roll a portion out on a lightly floured surface with a lightly floured rolling pin to 8 mm (⅜ inch) thick. Cut into heart shapes using an 8 cm (3¼ inch) cutter and arrange on the trays. Repeat with the remaining dough.

5  Bake for 12 minutes, swapping trays halfway through cooking, or until lightly browned around the edges. Leave on the trays to cool slightly, then transfer to a wire rack to cool completely.

6  Put the white chocolate in a small heatproof bowl over a saucepan of just simmering water, making sure the base of the bowl does not touch the water. Stir occasionally until the chocolate has melted.

7  Dip one half of each biscuit into the chocolate, allowing any excess to drip off. Place on a sheet of baking paper until the chocolate has set.

**Note:** These biscuits can be stored in an airtight container for up to 5 days.

# hot cross buns

**ENGLAND**  These spiced, sweet buns are part of the Easter tradition in many Christian countries. At one time in England they tried to ban the sale of the buns for religious reasons but they were too popular, so Queen Elizabeth I passed a law permitting them only at Easter time.

600 g (1 lb 5 oz/4 cups) white bread flour

1 teaspoon mixed (pumpkin pie) spice

1 teaspoon ground cinnamon

2 tablespoons caster (superfine) sugar

14 g (½ oz) dried yeast

40 g (1½ oz) butter

210 g (7½ oz/1⅔ cups) sultanas (golden raisins)

**paste for crosses**

35 g (1¼ oz/¼ cup) plain (all-purpose) flour

¼ teaspoon caster (superfine) sugar

**glaze**

1½ tablespoons caster (superfine) sugar

1 teaspoon gelatine

MAKES 12

1  Sift the flour and spices into a large bowl. Stir in the sugar and yeast. Rub in the butter with your fingertips. Stir in the sultanas. Make a well in the centre, then pour in 310 ml (10¾ fl oz/1¼ cups) lukewarm water. Stir with a wooden spoon and then your hands to make a soft dough. Turn the dough out onto a lightly floured surface and knead for 5 minutes, or until smooth, adding a little more flour if necessary.

2  Place the dough in a large floured bowl, cover with plastic wrap and leave in a warm, draught-free place for 40 minutes, or until doubled in size.

3  Preheat the oven to 200°C (400°F/Gas 6). Lightly grease a lamington tin. Turn the dough out onto a lightly floured surface and knead gently to deflate. Divide into 12 portions and roll each into a ball. Place the balls in the tin, just touching each other. Cover loosely with plastic wrap and leave in a warm, draught-free place for 20 minutes, or until nearly doubled in size.

4  To make the crosses, mix the flour, sugar and 2½ tablespoons water into a paste. Spoon into a freezer bag or zip-lock bag. Snip a small hole in one corner and pipe crosses on top of the buns.

5  Bake the buns in the oven for 20 minutes, or until golden brown and cooked through.

6  Meanwhile, put the sugar, gelatine and 1 tablespoon water in a small saucepan and stir over medium heat until dissolved. Brush over the hot buns and cool.

**Notes:** The dried fruit in these buns can be varied. Often, currants and chopped candied peel are used. The crosses are sometimes made with pastry instead of flour and water paste, or crosses can be scored into the dough prior to proving.

# baklava

**ARMENIA** Also a popular dessert in Greece, Turkey and Lebanon, baklava is thought to have been introduced by Armenian Christians who used 40 sheets of pastry to symbolise the 40 days of Lent. Traditionally, Armenian baklava is baked in a round pan and scored into a diamond pattern.

375 g (13 oz/3¾ cups) walnuts, finely chopped

155 g (5½ oz/1 cup) almonds, finely chopped

½ teaspoon ground cinnamon

½ teaspoon mixed (pumpkin pie) spice

1 tablespoon caster (superfine) sugar

16 sheets filo pastry

1½ tablespoons olive oil

250 g (9 oz) unsalted butter, melted

### syrup

165 g (5¾ oz/¾ cup) sugar

260 g (9¼ oz/¾ cup) honey

3 whole cloves

3 teaspoons freshly squeezed lemon juice

MAKES 16 PIECES

1 Preheat the oven to 180°C (350°F/Gas 4). Lightly grease the base and sides of a shallow 18 x 28 cm (7 x 11¼ inch) cake tin.

2 Mix together the walnuts, almonds, spices and sugar, then divide into three portions.

3 Working with one sheet of filo at a time (keep the rest covered with a dry tea towel (dish towel) and then a damp tea towel to prevent drying out), place a sheet of pastry on a kitchen bench. Mix the oil and melted butter and brush liberally over the pastry sheet. Fold the sheet in half crossways. Trim the edges so the pastry fits the base of the tin. Repeat with another three sheets of pastry, brushing each layer liberally with the butter mixture, and placing them over the base of the tin.

4 Sprinkle one portion of the nut filling over the pastry. Continue buttering the pastry, four sheets at a time, and layer with the nuts. Finish with a layer of pastry.

5 Trim the edges and brush the top with the remaining butter and oil. Use a knife to score lengthways into four portions. Bake for 30 minutes, or until golden and crisp.

6 To make the syrup, put the sugar, honey, cloves, lemon juice and 310 ml (10¾ fl oz/1¼ cups) water in a small saucepan and stir over low heat until the sugar has dissolved. Bring to the boil, then reduce the heat and simmer, without stirring, for 10 minutes, or until thickened. When the baklava is cooked, pour over the hot syrup. Set aside to cool. Serve cut into diamonds.

**Note:** Baklava can be stored for up to 5 days in an airtight container.

# fruit mince pies

**ENGLAND**  This dessert dates back to the Middle Ages, although then it was served as a savoury meat pie with spices and dried fruit to help preserve it so it would last longer. Traditionally served during the Christmas festive season they now contain a sweet fruit mince filling.

icing (confectioners') sugar, to dust

### pastry

300 g (10½ oz/2 cups) plain (all-purpose) flour

150 g (5½ oz) unsalted butter, chilled and cubed

85 g (3 oz/⅔ cup) icing (confectioners') sugar

2–3 tablespoons iced water

### fruit mince

55 g (2 oz/⅓ cup) chopped raisins

60 g (2¼ oz/⅓ cup) soft brown sugar

40 g (1½ oz/⅓ cup) sultanas (golden raisins)

40 g (1½ oz/¼ cup) mixed peel (mixed candied citrus peel)

1 tablespoon currants

1 tablespoon chopped almonds

1 small apple, grated

1 tablespoon freshly squeezed lemon juice

1 teaspoon finely grated orange zest

½ teaspoon mixed (pumpkin pie) spice

25 g (1 oz) unsalted butter, melted

MAKES 16

1  For the fruit mince, combine all the ingredients in a bowl. Cover and stand overnight.

2  Preheat the oven to 180°C (350°F/Gas 4). Lightly grease two 12-hole round-based patty pans.

3  To make the pastry, sift the flour into a bowl. Use your fingertips to rub in the butter until the mixture resembles fine breadcrumbs. Stir in the icing sugar and make a well in the centre. Add almost all of the iced water and mix with a flat-bladed knife, using a cutting action, until the mixture starts to come together in beads, adding the remaining water if necessary. Turn out onto a lightly floured surface and knead gently until just smooth. Divide into three equal portions.

4  With a lightly floured rolling pin, roll out a portion of the pastry until 3 mm (⅛ inch) thick. Using a 6 cm (2½ inch) round fluted cutter, cut out eight rounds. Press gently into the patty pan holes to line. Repeat with another portion of pastry to make another eight pastry cases.

5  Divide the fruit mince among the pastry cases. Roll out the remaining pastry as before until 2 mm (1/16 inch) thick. Using a 5 cm (2 inch) star cutter, cut out sixteen stars and place them on top of the pies.

6  Bake for 25 minutes or until the pastry is cooked through and golden. Stand the pies in the tins for 5 minutes, then carefully lift out and cool on a wire rack. Serve dusted lightly with the icing sugar.

# anzac biscuits

**AUSTRALIA** Anzac biscuits (cookies), or soldiers' biscuits, originated in 1915 (during World War I) when soldiers' wives and mothers would bake and send the biscuits to troops overseas. The biscuits were cheap to make and kept well as they contain no eggs or milk.

150 g (5½ oz/1 cup) plain (all-purpose) flour

165 g (5¾ oz/¾ cup) firmly packed brown sugar

100 g (3½ oz/1 cup) rolled (porridge) oats

90 g (3¼ oz/1 cup) desiccated coconut

125 g (4½ oz) unsalted butter, cubed

90 g (3¼ oz/¼ cup) golden syrup

1 teaspoon bicarbonate of soda (baking soda)

MAKES 24

1 Preheat the oven to 180°C (350°F/Gas 4). Line two baking trays with baking paper.

2 Sift the flour into a large bowl. Add the sugar, oats and coconut and make a well in the centre.

3 Put the butter and golden syrup in a small saucepan and stir over low heat until the butter has melted and the mixture is smooth. Remove from the heat. Dissolve the bicarbonate of soda in 1 tablespoon boiling water and add immediately to the butter mixture. It will foam up instantly. Add to the dry ingredients and stir with a wooden spoon until well combined.

4 Roll level tablespoons of the mixture into balls and place on the trays, allowing room for spreading. Flatten each biscuit slightly with your fingertips. Bake for 20 minutes, or until golden brown. Cool on trays for 5 minutes then transfer to a wire rack to cool completely.

**Note:** Anzac biscuits can be stored for up to 1 week in an airtight container.

# biscotti

**ITALY** First made in the Tuscany region of Italy, these crisp biscuits (cookies) have been around for centuries. The root words *bis* and *cotto* literally translate to twice and cooked, and refer exactly to the way these biscuits have been baked for generations.

410 g (14½ oz/2¾ cups) plain (all-purpose) flour, sifted

½ teaspoon baking powder

3 eggs, lightly beaten

165 g (5¾ oz/¾ cup) caster (superfine) sugar

½ teaspoon natural vanilla extract

150 g (5½ oz/1 cup) blanched almonds or pistachio nuts (or a mixture of both)

**MAKES ABOUT 30**

1 Preheat the oven to 180°C (350°F/Gas 4). Line two baking trays with baking paper. Sift together the flour and baking powder.

2 Use electric beaters to whisk the egg, sugar and vanilla until very thick and pale. Add the flour mixture and nuts and use a wooden spoon to mix to a soft dough. Turn out onto a lightly floured kitchen bench and divide the dough into two equal portions.

3 Roll each portion into a log about 20 cm (8 inches) long. Place on one of the trays and flatten slightly. Bake for 35 minutes, or until cooked through. Cool for 15 minutes. Reduce the oven temperature to 170°C (325°F/Gas 3).

4 Using a serrated knife, cut each log on the diagonal into 1 cm (½ inch) thick slices. Place on the baking trays. Bake for a further 15–20 minutes, or until the biscotti are pale golden and dry. Cool on wire racks.

# damper

**AUSTRALIA**  This Australian soda bread was made by stockmen, known as swagmen or drovers, who travelled into remote areas of bushland for weeks or months at a time with only basic rations to cook with. Damper was traditionally cooked in an open campfire.

450 g (1 lb/3 cups) self-raising flour, plus extra, for dusting

1 teaspoon salt

90 g (3¼ oz) unsalted butter, melted

125 ml (4 fl oz/½ cup) milk, plus extra, for glazing

butter and golden syrup, to serve

SERVES 8

1  Preheat the oven to 210°C (415°F/Gas 6–7). Lightly grease a baking tray.

2  Sift the flour and salt into a bowl and make a well in the centre. Combine the butter, milk and 160 ml (5¼ fl oz/¾ cup) water and add to the dry ingredients. Using a flat-bladed knife, stir until just combined.

3  Turn the dough out onto a lightly floured surface and knead for 20 seconds, or until smooth. Place the dough on the baking tray and press out to make a round with a 20 cm (8 inch) diameter.

4  Using a sharp-pointed knife, score the dough into eight sections, about 1 cm (½ inch) deep. Brush with a little extra milk and dust with the extra flour.

5  Bake for 10 minutes. Reduce the oven temperature to 180°C (350°F/Gas 4) and bake for a further 10 minutes, or until the damper is golden and sounds hollow when tapped on the base.

6  Serve warm or at room temperature, with butter and golden syrup.

# glossary

### Al dente
This is an Italian term that literally translates as 'to the tooth', which describes pasta that is cooked until it is tender but still firm to the bite.

### Angel hair pasta
Very thin, long strands of pasta, also known as capelli d'angelo. It tends to be thinner than vermicelli and is often shaped into 'nests'.

### Arborio rice
A short, fat rice that originated in Italy, which is used to make risottos because it holds its shape while creating a creamy texture when cooked.

### Basmati rice
A thin, long-grain rice with a nutty flavour, often used in Indian and Middle Eastern cooking. The name means 'fragrant'.

### Bean sprouts
These are the pale young shoots of the mung bean, often used in Asian cooking. The ends often need trimming and they should be kept in a plastic bag in the crisper section of the refrigerator for no longer than 3 days.

### Bocconcini
A fresh mozzarella cheese, usually sold in small balls and packed in whey or water. Bocconcini is an Italian word meaning 'mouthful'.

### Brioche
A soft French bread that has a deliciously rich, slightly sweet flavour. It is often eaten warm or used in puddings.

### Burghul (bulgur)
This is wheat grains that have been husked, parboiled, dried then cracked into a coarse grain. It is used extensively in Middle Eastern cooking and forms the basis of the well-known salad tabouleh (see page 132).

### Buttermilk
This is skim milk that has had a bacterial culture added to it to give it a slightly sour flavour and a thickened consistency. It is often used in pancakes and cakes to give them a light texture.

### Char siu
Chinese barbecued pork that has been marinated in a sweet and sour mixture and then roasted.

### Couscous
A cereal made from semolina — basically it is just tiny grains of pasta. It is a staple of North African cuisine and is used in both sweet and savoury dishes.

### Feta
A traditional Greek-style salty cheese that should be stored immersed in lightly salted water and kept in the refrigerator. Rinse and pat it dry before using.

### Filo pastry

A very thin pastry (almost like tissue paper) used in many sweet and savoury recipes from Greece and the Middle East. It is often brushed with butter and prepared in layers before baking. Baklava (see page 176) and Spanakopita (see page 104) are two well-known dishes made with filo pastry. It is available fresh or frozen.

### Fish sauce

This very strong smelling and fishy tasting condiment is made from the liquid from salted, fermented fish. It is used in Southeast Asian cooking much like salt is used to season dishes in Western cooking. It is called different things in different countries. Nuoc nam is the Vietnamese version and is the most commonly available.

### Fontina

A famous pale yellow Italian cow's milk cheese that is dotted with holes and has a mild, nutty flavour. It also melts easily, making it perfect to use in cooking.

### Fried bean curd

Cubes of bean curd, or tofu, that have been deep-fried; it has a crisp, golden skin and soft centre. It is great used in stir-fries and Asian-style soups.

### Ghee

This is a clarified butter that has been simmered until all the moisture has evaporated and the milk solids begin to brown. Ghee has a nutty, caramel flavour and is often used instead of butter or oil in Indian cooking.

### Gruyère

A Swiss cheese made from cow's milk with a rich, sweet, nutty flavour that is good for simply eating as it is or using in cooking.

### Haloumi

A semi-hard cheese from the Middle East. It has a salty flavour and a high melting point, which makes it perfect for grilling and for frying.

### Harissa

Originally from Tunisia in North Africa, harissa is a fiery hot sauce that is traditionally served with couscous or used to flavour soups and stews. Use just a little to start with and add more if you want to increase the heat.

### Hokkien noodles

Also known as hokkien mee, these thick, fresh egg noodles are popular in Chinese-style cooking.

### Jasmine rice

A long-grain aromatic rice from Thailand. It is popular in Thai, Chinese and other Southeast Asian cooking.

### Kaffir lime (makrut) leaves

These are the leaves from a citrus plant native to Southeast Asia. The double-tiered leaves are used in curries, soups and salads to add a hint of citrus flavour.

### Kecap manis

A thick, intensely flavoured, sweet soy sauce from Indonesia. If you can't find it, use regular soy sauce mixed with a little brown sugar.

### Kefalotyri cheese

A hard, salty, pale yellow cheese hailing from Greece and Cyprus and made from sheep's and/or goat's milk. Use Italian parmesan if you can't find it.

### Lemongrass

This herb is popular in Thai and Vietnamese cooking and imparts a lemony flavour to dishes such as stir-fries and curries. Chop or finely slice only the pale section before using. Alternatively, it can be pounded lightly and added as a whole piece to a slow-cooked dish — remove it at the end of cooking before serving.

## Madras curry powder

A fairly hot ground-spice mixture made from dried chillies, coriander seeds, cumin, mustard seeds, black peppercorns, curry leaves, ginger and turmeric. It originates from the south of India.

## Mirin

A sweet rice wine from Japan used in cooking. It adds sweetness and flavour to a range of dishes and sauces.

## Miso paste

This is actually a mixture of fermented tofu and grains that have been left to mature into a salty paste — similar to the consistency of peanut butter. Available in a variety of colours, flavours and textures, white and red being the most common, miso paste is used as a flavouring in Japanese cooking. It is also a good source of protein and B vitamins.

## Mortar and pestle

A mortar is a ceramic, stone, marble or wooden bowl. A pestle is a short, heavy baseball-bat-like implement. Together they are used to crush or grind foods, often spices and/or herbs, to make a powder or paste. Mortars and pestles are used all around the world and come in many different shapes and sizes.

## Mozzarella

A pale yellow, semi-soft cheese made from buffalo's or cow's milk and formed into round or pear shapes. It is popular in Italian cooking and often used for pizzas and lasagne as it becomes stringy when cooked. Fresh mozzarella is off-white in colour, has a softer texture and a sweet, delicate flavour.

## Nori

Thin sheets of dried seaweed. In Japanese cooking it is often used to wrap sushi and rice balls. It is sometimes finely cut and used as a seasoning or garnish.

## Oyster sauce

Originally from China, oyster sauce is made from soy sauce and dried oysters. It has a strong shellfish flavour and is a great addition to stir-fries and noodle dishes.

## Palm sugar

An unrefined sugar made from the sap of the sugar palm tree. It comes in two forms — either the texture of creamed or candied honey or in a solid, cake-like form that needs to be grated or finely chopped to be measured and used. It is traditionally used to sweeten foods in Indian and Asian cooking. Brown sugar can be used in its place if you can't find it.

## Parmesan

A hard Italian cheese that has a strong, sharp, distinctive flavour; it is made from cow's milk. You can buy pre-grated parmesan but, for the best flavour, it is best to buy it in a block and grate it yourself.

## Pickled ginger

Known in Japan as gari, this ginger has been thinly sliced and marinated in a mixture of sugar and vinegar. It is often served with Sushi rolls (see page 58).

## Rice paper rounds/wrappers

Edible, translucent, paper-thin sheets made from a paste of rice flour, tapioca flour, salt and water that is spread on bamboo mats and allowed to dry. (Have a look at the sheets and you will see the indented pattern from the woven bamboo.) Rice paper wrappers come in rounds and squares. They are always soaked briefly before using and are used to wrap foods to be eaten fresh or deep-fried.

## Rice vermicelli

Very thin rice noodles made from rice flour. They can either be softened in hot water or cooked briefly in boiling water before adding to dishes.

## Saffron threads

A fragrant spice used to flavour and tint food an orange colour. It is very expensive but only a small amount is needed as it is quite pungent.

## Savoiardi

Traditional Italian biscuits that are also known as lady fingers or sponge finger biscuits. They are traditionally used to make desserts such as Tiramisu (see page 153).

## Shaoxing rice wine

A traditional fermented wine made from rice. It is named after a famous wine-making city of the same name in China, and is used for cooking. It is sometimes called Chinese rice wine.

## Shiitake mushrooms

Brown-capped mushrooms with a strong meaty flavour originally from Japan and Korea. They are sometimes called Chinese black mushrooms.

## Shrimp paste

A firm paste, sold in blocks, that is used in Southeast Asian cooking. It is made from grinding up salted and fermented prawns (shrimp) — it has a strong salty, fishy flavour and is used in small quantities. When you open the packet, its smell can be very strong and almost offensive — but don't let this put you off using it. It needs to be cooked or toasted to mellow the aroma and flavour before you add it to your dish. The easiest way to do this is to wrap it in a piece of foil and place it under a preheated grill (broiler) for about 3 minutes each side or until it has a toasty, less pungent, aroma.

## Tabasco sauce

A fiery hot sauce made from very hot, small red chillies (that have been fermented for 3 years), salt and vinegar. It originated in the Mexican state of Tabasco. A small amount goes a long way, so use it sparingly.

## Tahini

A thick paste made from ground sesame seeds, with a texture like thin peanut butter. It is often used in Middle Eastern cooking and is used in making hummus (see page 36).

## Tamarind purée

Tamarinds are a native fruit in Asia, North Africa and India and are also known as Indian dates. The sour fruit pulp is sold as a concentrated purée, as a paste, or dried into bricks. It is often used in Middle Eastern and East Indian dishes as a flavouring much like lemon juice is used in Western cooking. It is also an important ingredient in Worcestershire sauce (see below).

## Vine leaves

Large green leaves of grape vines, mostly sold tinned and pickled in brine. They are used by Greek and Middle Eastern cooks to wrap food for cooking. They need to be drained and rinsed before using.

## Wasabi paste

Also called Japanese horseradish, wasabi paste comes from the root of an Asian plant. This green paste has a sharp, fiery, pungent flavour.

## Worcestershire sauce

This condiment was actually developed by the English while in India, but takes its name from Worcestershire, England, where it was first bottled. It is a pungent sauce that has an unusual combination of ingredients including garlic, soy sauce, tamarind, onion, molasses, lime, anchovies and vinegar.

# index

Published in 2011 by Murdoch Books Pty Limited

Murdoch Books Australia
Pier 8/9
23 Hickson Road
Millers Point NSW 2000
Phone: +61 (0) 2 8220 2000
Fax: +61 (0) 2 8220 2558
www.murdochbooks.com.au

Murdoch Books UK Limited
Erico House, 6th Floor
93–99 Upper Richmond Road
Putney, London SW15 2TG
Phone: +44 (0) 20 8785 5995
Fax: +44 (0) 20 8785 5985
www.murdochbooks.co.uk

Publisher: Kylie Walker
Project Editor and Food Editor: Anneka Manning
Editor: Jacqueline Blanchard
Concept Designer and Illustrator: Alex Frampton
Designer: Susanne Geppert
Production: Joan Beal
Photography: Michele Aboud (internals); Stuart Scott (cover, pages 2, 22, 38, 45, 166)
Stylist: Sarah DeNardi (internals); Sarah O'Brien (cover, pages 2, 22, 38, 45, 166)
Food Preparation: Julie Ray (internals); Grace Campbell (cover, pages 2, 22, 38, 45, 166)

National Library of Australia Cataloguing-in-Publication entry
Author: Murdoch Books Test Kitchen.
Title: I want to be a chef: around the world / Murdoch Books Test Kitchen.
ISBN: 9781741969764 (pbk.)
Notes: Includes index.
Subject: Cooking
Dewey Number: 641.5
A catalogue reference is available for this book from the British Library.

Printed by C & C Offset in China. Printed in 2011.

IMPORTANT: Those who might be at risk from the effects of salmonella poisoning (the elderly, pregnant women, young children and those suffering from immune deficiency diseases) should consult their doctor with any concerns about eating raw eggs.

CONVERSION GUIDE: You may find cooking times vary depending on the oven you are using. For fan-forced ovens, as a general rule, set the oven temperature to 20°C (35°F) lower than indicated in the recipe. We have used 20 ml (4 teaspoon) tablespoon measures. If you are using a 15 ml (3 teaspoon) tablespoon add an extra teaspoon of the ingredient for each tablespoon specified.